Cyberbullying

From the beginning of 2000, with the increase and diffusion of modern technologies, a new form of bullying using electronic means has emerged. Literature has reached some consistent findings on the description of the problem. However, there is still a lack of knowledge about developmental processes of cyberbullying and about possible predictors and correlates. Some of the main emerging areas investigated in connection with cyberbullying are: personality factors, callous unemotional traits and self-control, memory cognitive distortions, emotional and moral mechanisms, ICT use and media exposure, family and social contexts.

Another important issue is the relation between cyberbullying and face to face bullying. To this regards, from face to face literature we know some of the mechanisms in the peer group such as the relation between bullying, dominance and popularity and the role of bystanders in the social dynamic of the attacks. However, nothing is known about the cyber community. Contributions of this volume attempt to investigate these group mechanisms in the cyber community. Finally, for the victims, long-term consequences are also relevant, both in terms of perceived stress level and of the association between cyber-victimization and mental health.

This special issue offers important new findings on the development and consequences of cyberbullying and cyber-victimization, and opens new and future directions of research.

Ersilia Menesini is Professor of Developmental Psychology and Educational Psychology at the University of Florence, Italy.

Christiane Spiel is Professor of Educational Psychology at the University of Vienna, Austria.

T0347538

Cyberbullying

Development, consequences, risk and protective factors

A Special Issue of the European Journal of Developmental Psychology

Edited by

Ersilia Menesini and Christiane Spiel

 **Psychology Press**
Taylor & Francis Group

First published 2012
by Psychology Press Ltd
27 Church Road, Hove, East Sussex BN3 2FA, UK

www.psypress.com

Simultaneously published in the USA and Canada
by Taylor & Francis Inc
711 Third Avenue, New York, NY 10017
First issued in paperback 2014

Psychology Press is an imprint of the Taylor and Francis Group, an informa business

British Library Cataloguing in Publication Data
A catalogue record for this book is available from the British Library

ISBN 978-1-84872-762-5 (hbk)
ISBN 978-1-138-84486-5 (pbk)
ISSN 1740-5629 (print) / 1740-5610 (online)

Typeset in Times New Roman
by Taylor & Francis Books

Publisher's Note
The publisher would like to make readers aware that the chapters in this book may be referred to as articles as they are identical to the articles published in the special issue. The publisher accepts responsibility for any inconsistencies that may have arisen in the course of preparing this volume for print.

Contents

CONTENTS

Citation information

The chapters in this book were originally published in the *European Journal of Developmental Psychology*, volume 9, issue 2 (2012). When citing this material, please use the original page numbering for each article, as follows:

Chapter 1
Introduction: Cyberbullying: Development, consequences, risk and protective factors
Ersilia Menesini and Christiane Spiel
European Journal of Developmental Psychology, volume 9, issue 2 (2012)
pp. 163-167

Chapter 2
A longitudinal study of cyberbullying: Examining risk and protective factors
Kostas A. Fanti, Andreas G. Demetriou, and Veronica V. Hawa
European Journal of Developmental Psychology, volume 9, issue 2 (2012)
pp. 168-181

Chapter 3
Recalling unpresented hostile words: False memories predictors of traditional and cyberbullying
Manila Vannucci, Annalaura Nocentini, Giuliana Mazzoni, and
Ersilia Menesini
European Journal of Developmental Psychology, volume 9, issue 2 (2012)
pp. 182-194

Chapter 4
Cyberbullying and traditional bullying in adolescence: Differential roles of moral disengagement, moral emotions, and moral values
Sonja Perren and Eveline Gutzwiller-Helfenfinger
European Journal of Developmental Psychology, volume 9, issue 2 (2012)
pp. 195-209

Introduction: Cyberbullying: Development, consequences, risk and protective factors

Ersilia Menesini[1] and Christiane Spiel[2]

[1]Department of Psychology, University of Florence, Florence, Italy
[2]Faculty of Psychology, University of Vienna, Vienna, Austria

With the increase and diffusion of modern technologies a new form of bullying has emerged among children and adolescents. Many researchers define it as *cyberbullying, electronic bullying* or *internet bullying*. With these terms we refer to voluntary and repeated assaults against a person through electronic means. These attacks can be: offensive e-mails or text messages; insults through chat rooms or instant messaging; photos or videos on mobile or web; exclusion from social networks or appropriation of others' credentials and identity information.

Studies on cyberbullying are relatively recent, mainly published in the last ten years. These contributions have been focused on a first description of the phenomenon in relation to the medium used (mobile phone or internet) and on the possible link between traditional bullying and cyberbullying. As a global picture cyberbullying represents a threatening experience among young people in different Western countries, although it is showing different levels of prevalence in relation to different cultures, contexts and personal characteristics. From recent estimation, the percentages of children and adolescents involved in the problem can reach values close to 10% of 9- to 16-year-olds in Europe (Livingstone, Haddon, Görzig, & Ólafsson, with EU Kids Online Network, 2011) as well as in North America (Englander, 2010; Ybarra, Diener-West, & Leaf, 2007). Some children reported to be cyber-victims, some others cyberbullies, yet others take both roles.

Correspondence should be addressed to Ersilia Menesini, Department of Psychology, University of Florence, Via S. Salvi, 12 50135 Firenze, Italy. E-mail: ersilia.menesini@unifi.it

© 2012 Psychology Press, an imprint of the Taylor & Francis Group, an Informa business
http://www.psypress.com/edp   http://dx.doi.org/10.1080/17405629.2011.652833

Most studies have emphasized the overlap between cyber- and face-to-face bullying (Ybarra et al., 2007), demonstrating how victims and bullies in one context are involved also in another one. Those who bully at school have a higher probability of being a cyberbully in the virtual environment and a similar picture has been reported for victims (Gradinger, Strohmeier, & Spiel, 2009). But it also appears that a certain percentage of those who are victims online do not report being bullied at school. This result suggests that electronic bullying is not always an extension of traditional bullying, and that some features make the cyberbullies and the cyber-victims different from the traditional bullies and victims (Smith et al., 2008). Internet and other new technologies may have increased the chances for harassment for youth who might otherwise not be targeted. Probably for a proportion of the cyber-victims the use of new forms of multimedia technology has created a vulnerability that they may not have typically experienced elsewhere (David-Ferdon & Feldman Hertz, 2007).

Still, in relation to the necessity to compare cyber- and traditional bullying, studies have focused on the definition and measurement issues, trying to understand whether some criteria relevant of face-to-face bullying can also be applied to cyberbullying (Dooley, Pyzalsky, & Cross, 2009; Gradinger, Strohmeier, & Spiel, 2010; Menesini, Nocentini, & Calussi, 2011; Nocentini et al., 2010).

The influence of age and gender has been also investigated. Findings concerning gender are mixed. Kowalsky and Limber (2007) found that females are more involved in cyberbullying than males. The indirect characteristic of the electronic bullying may explain the female preference for this type of aggression. The authors also found that fewer gender differences were observed across the methods used to bully electronically than for the forms of traditional bullying. These results are confirmed but are also denied from other studies. Qing Li (2006) has in fact found a greater male than a female involvement, while some others authors, like Slonje and Smith (2008) found no significant gender differences. Furthermore, the method used to bully electronically was sometimes shown to be related to gender, with the girls preferring instant messaging, e-mail or chatrooms, and boys using more photos or videos posted online (Menesini et al., 2011). Studies on the age influence showed highest prevalence rates of cyberbullying during adolescence. This is explained not only by the capacity of adolescents to be able to use new technologies, often better than adults, but also because at this age the use of new technology provides additional opportunities for socialization (Valkenburg & Peter, 2011).

Although some consistent findings have been reached so far, there is still a lack of knowledge about developmental processes of cyberbullying and on possible predictors and correlates, such as: personality and social factors, ICT use and media exposure, family or social contexts representing risk or protective factors. Furthermore, having in mind young people's well-being, knowledge about the consequences of cyerbullying or cyber-victimization is needed.

The eight papers in this special issue try to give answers to these challenging questions. The paper by Fanti, Demetriou, and Hawa (pp. 168–181) offers an important contribution to the development of cyberbullying in comparison to traditional bullying. The paper illustrates that by adopting a more systemic approach we can understand the ecological development of cyerbullying, and to what extent it is influenced by personality factors, by violent media exposure, and mediated by family support and monitoring.

Another emerging question concerns the correlates of cyberbullying and to what extent they are similar or different to correlates of traditional bullying. Research on risk factors suggests the importance of paying attention to the concept of information processing. Particularly, we need to know which and to what extent cognitive mechanisms can be related to cyberbullying. The paper by Vannucci, Nocentini, Mazzoni, and Menesini (pp. 182–194) offers an interesting direction of investigation, i.e., the underlying role of memory distortions. If a child is involved in violent and threatening situations is he or she more inclined to produce hostile false memories in neutral contexts also? Results support this hypothesis showing that violent false memories were positively associated with cyberbullying and with traditional bullying.

Other relevant cognitive and emotional mechanisms often reported in the literature on violence and antisocial behaviour are connected to morality and to mechanisms of self-control. In the first case we know that values, moral disengagement and lack of guilt in violent situations are related to aggressive and antisocial behaviour. Can we also expect similar mechanisms in the case of online attacks? The paper by Perren and Gutzwiller-Helfenfinger (pp. 195–209) offers a nice answer to this issue showing that a lack of moral values and a lack of remorse predicted both traditional and cyberbullying behaviour.

In relation to personality factors, low self-control can be a relevant factor that impacts on cyberbullying and cyber-victimization among adolescents in a similar way to the case of antisocial and delinquent behaviour. The paper by Vazsonyi, Machackova, Sevcikova, Smahel, and Cerna (pp. 210–227) addresses this problem with a study carried out in 25 European countries. Beyond cultural differences, results show positive associations between online and offline bullying behaviours (perpetration and victimization), and direct as well as indirect effects by low self-control on cyberbullying perpetration and victimization.

Usually bullies want to gain status and popularity in the peer group whereas a strong correlate of traditional victimization is low popularity. So far, there is a lack of knowledge whether the same pattern exists for cyberbullying and cyber-victimization. In particular, it is of interest whether popularity is a potential antecedent or a consequence of both traditional victimization and cyber victimization. These are some issues addressed by Gradinger, Strohmeier, Schiller, Stefanek, and Spiel (pp. 228–243), who show that cyber-victimization is neither stable during a one-year period, nor could it be predicted by traditional victimization, popularity or perceived popularity. Instead, cyber-victimization fosters popularity in girls.

Usually in face-to-face interactions, bystanders may take a role to support the bully or more rarely to defend the victim. However, nothing is known so far about the cyber community. Can we find similar roles? How can other persons take part? Do they observe, diffuse or actively join in the cyber attack? Do they feel responsible or show remorse for what has been done? The paper by Slonje, Smith, and Frisén (pp. 244–259) addresses this problem and shows that cyberbullies express less remorse than traditional bullies.

Long-term consequences of electronic bullying are also relevant to understanding the nature and the development of cyberbullying. Three papers in the special issue have a longitudinal design but only two specifically address the consequences of online victimization and bullying. The paper by Staude-Müller, Hansen, and Voss (pp. 260–274) highlights how stressful the experience of victimization can be and that both the characteristics of the victim and the properties of the incident can be identified as predictors of distress. Specifically, personality characteristics, such as higher neuroticism, chronic stress, and prior experiences of online victimization correlate with stronger stress. The paper by Dooley, Shaw, and Cross (pp. 275–289) addresses the association between cyber-victimization and mental health taking into consideration young people's need for effective coping strategies. The study shows that students who respond aggressively use significantly fewer assertive strategies, have more conduct and hyperactivity problems, more overall difficulties, and fewer prosocial behaviours than students who respond assertively but not aggressively.

We conclude that this special issue offers important new findings on the development and consequences of cyberbullying and cyber-victimization and opens new and future directions of research.

REFERENCES

David-Ferdon, C., & Feldman Hertz, M. (2007). Electronic media, violence, and adolescents: An emerging public health problem. *Journal of Adolescent Health, 41*, 1–5.

Dooley, J. J., Pyzalsky, J., & Cross, D. (2009). Cyberbullying versus face-to-face bullying—A theoretical and conceptual review. *Zeitschrift für Psychologie/Journal of Psychology, 217*(4), 182–188.

Englander, E. K. (2010). Editorial for the special issue on cyberbullying. *Journal of Social Sciences, 6*(4), 508–509.

Gradinger, P., Strohmeier, D., & Spiel, C. (2009). Traditional bullying and cyberbullying: Identification of risk groups for adjustment problems. *Zeitschrift für Psychologie/Journal of Psychology, 217*, 205–213.

Gradinger, P., Strohmeier, D., & Spiel, C. (2010). Definition and measurement of cyberbullying. *Cyberpsychology: Journal of Psychosocial Research on Cyberspace, 4*(2), Article 1. (Available at: http://cyberpsychology.eu/view.php?cisloclanku=2010112301&article=1)

Kowalski, R. M., & Limber, S. P. (2007). Electronic bullying among middle school students. *Journal of Adolescent Health, 41*, 22–30.

Li, Q. (2006). Cyberbullying in schools: A research of gender differences. *School Psychology International, 27*, 157–170.

Livingstone, S., Haddon, L., Görzig, A., & Ólafsson, K., with members of the EU Kids Online Network. (2011). *Risks and safety on the internet. The perspective of European children. Full findings and policy implications from the EU Kids Online survey of 9–16 year olds and their parents in 25 countries.* (Retrieved from: http://www2.lse.ac.uk/media@lse/research/EU KidsOnline/EUKidsII%20(2009–11)/EUKidsOnlineIIReports/D4FullFindings.pdf)

Menesini, E., Nocentini, A., & Calussi, P. (2011). The measurement of cyberbullying: Dimensional structure and relative item severity and discrimination. *Cyberpsychology & Behavior, 14*(5), 267–274.

Nocentini, A., Calmaestra, J., Schultze-Krumbholz, A., Scheithauer, H., Ortega, R., & Menesini, E. (2010). Cyberbullying: Labels, behaviours and definition in three European countries. *Australian Journal of Guidance and Counselling, 20*(2), 129–142.

Slonje, R., & Smith, P. K. (2008). Cyberbullying: Another main type of bullying? *Scandinavian Journal of Psychology, 49*, 147–154.

Smith, P. K., Mahdavi, J., Carvalho, M., Fisher, S., Russell, S., & Tippett, N. (2008). Cyberbullying: Its nature and impact in secondary school pupils. *Journal of Child Psychology and Psychiatry, 49*, 376–385.

Valkenburg, P. N., & Peter, J. (2011). Online communication among adolescents: An integrated model of its attraction, opportunities, and risks. *Journal of Adolescent Health, 48*, 121–127.

Ybarra, M. L., Diener-West, M., & Leaf, P. J. (2007). Examining the overlap in internet harassment and school bullying: Implications for school intervention. *Journal of Adolescent Health, 41*, 42–50.

A longitudinal study of cyberbullying: Examining risk and protective factors

Kostas A. Fanti, Andreas G. Demetriou, and Veronica V. Hawa

Department of Psychology, University of Cyprus, Nicosia, Cyprus

The objective of the current study was to examine possible risk (school-bullying and victimization, exposure to media violence, callous-unemotional traits, impulsivity and narcissism) and protective (family, peer and school social support) factors that might be associated with cyberbullying and cyber-victimization by employing a longitudinal, two-wave design. The sample consisted of 1,416 (50.1% girls) adolescents living in Cyprus. The findings suggested cross-sectional and longitudinal associations between school-bullying and cyberbullying and between school-victimization and cyber-victimization. Furthermore, callous-unemotional traits were longitudinally related to cyberbullying. Media violence exposure was a risk factor leading to both cyberbullying and cyber-victimization, while family social support was a protective factor for both types of adjustment problems. Finally, family social support protected adolescents living in single-parent households from being cyber-victimized when their friendships were not supportive.

Keywords: Cyberbullying; Cyber-victimization; Psychopathic traits; Social support; Media violence exposure.

Bullying is an international, widespread phenomenon occurring in different social contexts, such as the schoolyard, the workplace, and more recently technology. The majority of research investigating bullying behaviour has been focusing on school-bullying, which is defined as repeated physical, verbal or psychological attack or intimidation that is intended to cause fear, distress or harm to the victim (Olweus, 1993). Nowadays with the rapid

Correspondence should be addressed to Kostas A. Fanti, Department of Psychology, University of Cyprus, PO Box 20537, CY 1678, Nicosia, Cyprus. E-mail: kfanti@ucy.ac.cy

The research leading to these results has received funding from the European Community's Seventh Framework Program (FP7-PEOPLE-2007-4-3-IRG) under Grant Agreement No. 224903.

increase in electronic or online communication and the increase use of computers and mobile phones by young people, bullying is no longer limited to the schoolyard (Juvonen & Gross, 2008). Even though prior studies have provided evidence for an overlap between school-bullying and cyberbullying (Beran & Li, 2005; Li, 2007), cyberbullying differs from school-bullying in that it allows for limitless boundaries, an infinite audience, and the anonymity of the perpetrator (Patchin & Hinduja, 2006).

Cyberbullying is defined as an aggressive, intentional act carried out by an individual or a group of individuals with the use of electronic forms of contact (Smith et al., 2008). This action is repeated across time and the victim cannot easily defend him- or herself (Strom & Strom, 2005). Cyberbullies may harass, tease, disrespect, or exclude from social activities fellow peers with the use of instant messaging, chat rooms, e-mail, and text messages through cell phones and computers (Swartz, 2009). In order to understand the development of cyberbullying and cyber-victimization, the current study utilized an ecological approach by taking into account adolescents' personality characteristics and the social contexts in which adolescents are embedded (Bronfenbrenner, 1979).

On the individual level, we consider three personality traits, callous-unemotional (CU) traits, narcissism, and impulsivity. Research suggests that the presence of these personality traits designates an important subgroup of antisocial youth or youth with conduct problems (Frick & Dickens, 2006). Among youth with conduct problems, those high on CU traits (e.g., lack of remorse or guilt; lack of concern for others' feelings; and shallow or deficient emotions) show a more severe, aggressive, and stable pattern of antisocial behaviour (Frick & White, 2008). According to Fanti, Frick, and Georgiou (2009), CU traits are also associated with school-bullying but not victimization. CU traits constitute the affective dimension of psychopathy; psychopathy comprises two other dimensions, narcissism and impulsivity, each of which has been linked with aggressive behaviour in youth (Frick & Hare, 2001). Compared with non-involved youth, school victims and bullies are at greater risk of displaying impulsive behaviour (O'Brennan, Bradshaw, & Sawyer, 2009; Olweus, 1995). Narcissism was found to be positively related to bullying behaviour (Ang, Ong, Lim, & Lim, 2010), and narcissistic youth tend to perceive themselves as victims of others' interpersonal transgressions more so than other youth (McCullough, Emmons, Kilpatrick, & Mooney, 2003). In the current study, we attempted to apply the rich body of literature on conduct problems, aggression and school-bullying to cyberbullying and cyber-victimization in an effort to improve our understanding of the development of this new form of bullying. It was expected that CU traits would have the power to influence the development of cyberbullying and that narcissism and impulsivity would influence both cyberbullying and cyber-victimization.

In terms of environmental influences, we posited that media violence exposure (MVE) would be a risk marker for both cyberbullying and cyber-victimization. MVE may lead to desensitization to real-life aggression and to the suffering of victims, which increases the likelihood of aggressive behaviour (Fanti, Vanman, Henrich, & Avraamides, 2009). Additionally, cyberbullying is a form of bullying behaviour that takes place with the use of different media, such as the internet, suggesting that MVE might be especially detrimental for this type of behaviour. Also, prior research has provided evidence for the association between exposure to television and school-bullying and cyberbullying (Calvete, Orue, Estévez, Villardón & Padilla 2010; Kuntsche et al., 2006; Zimmerman, Glew, Christakis, & Katon, 2005), although it is unclear how MVE is associated with different forms of victimization; an objective of the current study.

In understanding development, one must consider not only risk processes but also how the environment protects adolescents from developing maladaptive behaviours (Sroufe & Rutter, 1984). The current study took into account three protective variables in the child's proximal environment, family, school and friend social support. Empirical evidence suggested that positive school climate and friend social support are negatively related to verbal, physical and cyberbullying (Williams & Guerra, 2007). A supportive school climate and a supportive social network of peers may also protect children from being victimized (Eliot, Cornell, Gregory, & Fa, 2010; Pellegrini & Bartini, 2000). Parental support has been associated with less involvement in all forms of bullying including cyberbullying (Wang, Iannotti, & Nansel, 2009). In the present study, it was expected that youth who experience support from school personnel, family members, and peers would be less likely to engage in cyberbullying and less likely to experience cyber-victimization. This hypothesis is based on the ecological approach, which proposes that multiple social contexts, in which youth are embedded simultaneously, work together to influence adjustment (Brookmeyer, Fanti, & Henrich, 2006). The intersecting social ecologies of family, friend and school are also expected to interact with one another to influence cyberbullying and cyber-victimization.

Last, gender and family structure differences will be taken into account. Prior work has suggested that females are more likely to report being cyberbullied than their male peers and that boys use cyberbullying to a greater extent than girls (Calvete et al., 2010; Li, 2007). However, Finn (2004) did not report any significant gender differences among cyberbullies and cyber-victims. Moreover, youth from single-parent families are at greater risk for exhibiting aggressive behaviour and for being victimized by peers in comparison to youth from intact families (Grifin, Botvin, Scheier, Diaz, & Miller, 2000; Turner, Finkelhor, & Ormrod, 2007).

In summary, the aim of the present study was to examine possible risk and protective factors that might be associated with cyberbullying and cyber-victimization, a field of inquiry that has received little empirical attention. In accordance with the ecological model, MVE and psychopathic personality traits were hypothesized to place a child at risk for the development of cyberbullying and cyber-victimization. However, experiencing support from family, peer, and school members was expected to protect children from engaging in these behaviours. The role of gender and family structure was also taken into consideration.

METHOD

Participants

The sample consisted of 1,416 adolescents living in Cyprus (50.1% girls; aged 11–14 years at the first assessment, $M_{age} = 12.89$, $SD = 0.78$). Following approval of the study by the Cyprus Ministry of Education, 13 middle schools were randomly selected (12 public, 1 private) from three of the four school districts (Lefkosia, Larnaca, Lemeso) in Cyprus. After approval of the study by the school boards, students were given an informed consent form for their parents to sign. In the classroom, students were informed about the study and were also informed about their rights as participants. Only students with parental consent were permitted to participate in the study. Group assessments were conducted with questionnaires being administered by trained research assistants. Prior to the first assessment, parental consent was obtained from 1,513 students, and these students completed questionnaires administered during Year 1. At the second assessment one year later, 93.59% ($n = 1,416$) of the original sample of students participated. Attrition was due to an inability to contact students who had moved away or transferred to a different school. The sample was diverse in terms of parental educational levels (20.1% did not complete high school, 46% had a high-school education, and 33.9% had a university degree) and parental marital status (7.2% of the families consisted of one-parent households).

Measures

Psychopathic traits. CU traits were measured with the Inventory of Callous-Unemotional Traits (ICU; Frick, 2004), which is a 24-item self-report scale. Narcissism (seven items) and impulsivity (five items) were measured with the Antisocial Process Screening Device–Youth report (APSD; Frick & Hare, 2001). All the items were placed on a 4-point scale (from $0 = $ *Not at all true* to $3 = $ *Definitely true*). The items measuring CU traits ($\alpha = .80$; e.g., "I do not show my emotions to others"), narcissism

($\alpha = .70$; e.g., "I act charming or nice to get things I want"), and impulsivity ($\alpha = .73$; e.g., "I do not plan ahead or I leave things until the last moment") formed internally consistent scales. Previous research has provided evidence for the validity of the self-reported versions of the ICU and APSD in community and high risk samples in Cyprus, Germany and the USA (Fanti et al., 2009; Kimonis, Frick, Skeem, Marsee, Cruise, Munoz, Aucoin, & Morris, 2008; Munoz & Frick, 2007).

MVE. Participants were asked five questions regarding the average time per week (ranging from 0 to more than 20 hours per week) they spent watching violent television programmes, violent scenes on the internet, violent movies (at home or in movie theatres), and playing violent video games ($\alpha = .89$). This questionnaire was based on prior work by Funk, Bechtoldt-Baldacci, Pasold, and Baumgartner (2004).

Supportive social relations. These were assessed with the Multidimensional Scale of Perceived Social Support (MSPSS; Zimet, Dahlem, Zimet, & Farley, 1988). This instrument was used to measure supportive relationships within three contexts: family ($\alpha = .82$; e.g., "I get the emotional support I need from my family"), friend ($\alpha = .80$; e.g., "I can count on my friend when things go wrong"), and school ($\alpha = .87$; e.g., "The staff at my school provides me the support and encouragement that I need"). The participants respondent on a 4-point scale (from $0 = Not\ at\ all\ true$ to $3 = Definitely\ true$). Prior work has provided evidence that the MSPSS is a valid and reliable measure of perceived social support during adolescence (Canty-Mitchell & Zimet, 2000).

Bullying, victimization, cyberbullying, and cyber-victimization. The Student Survey of Bullying Behaviour-Revised (SSBB-R; Varjas, Meyers, & Hunt, 2006) was administered at Years 1 and 2 to measure school-bullying, school-victimization, cyberbullying and cyber-victimization. Participants indicated whether they had engaged in different types of bullying or how often they experienced different types of victimization on an ordinal scale of: *never, once or twice a year, monthly, weekly,* or *daily.* The SSBB-R includes 12 items assessing school-bullying ($\alpha = .89$; e.g., "How often do you pick on younger, smaller, less powerful, or less popular kids by hitting or kicking them?"), 12 items assessing school victimization ($\alpha = .90$; e.g., "How often do older, bigger, more popular or more powerful kids pick on you by hitting or kicking you?"), four items assessing cyberbullying ($\alpha = .86$), and four items assessing cyber-victimization ($\alpha = .91$). To asses cyberbullying and cyber-victimization participants were asked how often they *sent* or *received* a threatening or harassing: (1) e-mail; (2) instant message; (3) message in a chat room or social networking sites; and (4) Short Text Message (SMS).

Previous research using the SSBB-R successfully measured school-bullying, school-victimization, cyberbullying, and cyber-victimization in community samples of adolescents in Cyprus and the USA (Fanti et al., 2009; Hunt, Meyers, Jarrett, & Neel, 2005; Varjas et al., 2006).

RESULTS

Descriptive statistics

Table 1 reports the descriptive statistics of the study's variables measured at Times 1 and 2 and the correlations among the variables under investigation. School-bullying and victimization and cyberbullying and victimization were correlated cross-sectionally and longitudinally. Furthermore, cyberbullying and cyber-victimization were positively associated with the three dimensions of psychopathy and MVE, while they were negatively correlated with family and friend social support, providing initial evidence of potential risk and protective variables. According to independent samples t-tests, boys scored higher than girls on school-bullying, $t(1415) = 8.04$, $p < .001$, and victimization, $t(1415) = 4.90$, $p < .001$, CU traits, $t(1415) = 8.06$, $p < .001$, narcissism, $t(1415) = 6.65$, $p < .001$, impulsivity, $t(1415) = 16.03$, $p < .001$, MVE, $t(1415) = 16.70$, $p < .001$, Time 1 cyberbullying, $t(1415) = 7.39$, $p < .001$, and cyber-victimization, $t(1415) = 4.55$, $p < .001$, Time 2 cyberbullying, $t(1415) = 6.28$, $p < .001$, and cyber-victimization, $t(1415) = 3.33$, $p = .001$, and lower on friend social support, $t(1415) = 9.03$, $p < .001$. According to paired-sample t-tests, there was a significant mean-level increase in cyber-victimization from Year 1 to Year 2, $t(1415) = 2.40$, $p < .05$. No change in cyberbullying was identified, $t(1415) = 0.83$, $p = .41$.

Hierarchical linear regressions

Table 2 shows the hierarchical linear regression analyses with cyberbullying and cyber-victimization as the outcomes. In step 1, we controlled for demographics—gender (coded with 0 for boys and 1 for girls), and parental marital status (coded with 0 for one-parent families and 1 for intact families). In step 2 we controlled for Year 1 cyberbullying, cyber-victimization, school-bullying and school victimization. Step 3 included all the risk variables (MVE, CU traits, narcissism, and impulsivity) and step 4 the protective variables (family, friend, and school social support). Subsequent steps included the two-way and three-way interactions between social-support variables. Interactions between the demographic variables (gender and parental marital status) and all the variables under investigation as well as the two- and three-way interactions between social support variables were also examined. To probe the interaction effects we used the

TABLE 1
Descriptive statistics and correlations among the main study variables

						Time 1						Time 2	
	CU	NAR	IMP	SB	SV	FamS	FrS	SchS	MVE	CB	CV	CB	CV
NAR	.30**												
IMP	.33**	.60**											
SB	.36**	.51**	.46**										
SV	.15**	.31**	.33**	.49**									
FamS	−.38**	−.19**	−.25**	−.22**	−.23**								
FrS	−.32**	−.03	−.07**	−.10**	−.22**	.35**							
SchS	−.28**	−.10**	−.24**	−.16**	−.15**	.38**	.38**						
MVE	.21**	.26**	.31**	.28**	.14**	−.11**	−.06**	−.09**					
CB Time 1	.29**	.21**	.16**	.48**	.29**	−.21**	−.11**	−.01	.38**				
CV Time 1	.21**	.17**	.17**	.32**	.39**	−.18**	−.08**	−.01	.30**	.67**			
CB Time 2	.14**	.15**	.12**	.17**	.08**	−.12**	−.06**	−.04	.41**	.40**	.28**		
CV Time 2	.12**	.18**	.15**	.17**	.18**	−.18**	−.07**	−.05	.35**	.24**	.35**	.72**	
Descriptives	M (SD)	M (SD)	M (SD)	M (SD)	M (SD)	M (SD)	M (SD)	M (SD)	M (SD)	M (SD)	M (SD)	M (SD)	M (SD)
Boys	22.18 (8.81)	6.16 (3.78)	5.65 (3.23)	6.72 (8.16)	10.03 (9.93)	8.93 (2.81)	7.12 (2.82)	5.26 (3.33)	1.72 (1.57)	0.84 (2.51)	0.83 (2.29)	1.01 (2.73)	0.98 (2.41)
Girls	18.53 (8.29)	4.91 (3.33)	4.54 (2.77)	3.75 (5.68)	7.65 (8.31)	9.16 (2.96)	8.46 (2.80)	5.55 (3.40)	0.58 (0.89)	0.21 (1.03)	0.49 (1.46)	0.19 (1.04)	0.48 (1.49)

Notes: $N = 1,416$. **$p < .01$; *$p < .05$. CU = callous-unemotional traits; NAR = narcissism; IMP = impulsivity; SB = school bullying; SV = school victimization; FamS = family social support; FrS = friend social support; SchS = school social support; MVE = media violence exposure; CB = cyberbullying; CV = cyber-victimization.

TABLE 2
Regression analyses with Year 2 cyberbullying and cyber-victimization as the outcomes

	Time 2 cyberbullying				Time 2 cyber-victimization			
	B	$SE\ B$	β	ΔR^2	B	$SE\ B$	β	ΔR^2
Step 1				.04**				.02**
Gender	−0.83	0.11	−0.20**		−0.51	0.11	−0.13**	
Family structure	−0.05	0.23	−0.01		−0.57	0.22	−0.07*	
Step 2				.12**				.11**
School victimization	−0.01	0.01	−0.04		0.02	0.01	0.10*	
School bullying	0.04	0.01	0.16**		0.02	0.01	0.01	
Cyber-victimization	0.05	0.04	0.06		0.21	0.03	0.24**	
Cyberbullying	0.39	0.04	0.37**		0.01	0.04	0.01	
Step 3				.04**				.02**
Media violence exposure	0.21	0.05	0.16**		0.11	0.04	0.10**	
CU traits	0.02	0.01	0.11**		0.01	0.01	0.04	
Narcissism	−0.01	0.03	−0.01		0.05	0.03	0.06	
Impulsivity	−0.01	0.03	−0.02		−0.02	0.02	−0.03	
Step 4				.01**				.01*
Family social support	−0.05	0.02	−0.10**		−0.04	0.02	−0.10**	
Friend social support	0.01	0.02	0.02		−0.01	0.02	−0.01	
School social support	0.01	0.02	0.01		0.01	0.01	0.02	
Step 5 (two-way interactions)								.01**
Marital status × Family social support					0.16	0.04	0.44**	
Family × Friend social support					0.01	0.01	0.09*	
Step 6 (three-way interactions)								.01**
Marital status × Family × Friend social support					−0.01	0.01	−0.34**	

Notes: $N = 1,416$. **$p < .01$; *$p < .05$. Regression coefficients represent value at initial entry. All the independent variables were measured at Time 1.

procedures described by Aiken and West (1991). All variables were centred to facilitate ease of interpretation of the significant interaction terms. Table 2 only reports the significant interactions.

Cyberbullying. Table 2 shows the hierarchical linear regression analysis with cyberbullying as the dependent variable. In the first step of independent variables, gender was significantly associated with cyberbullying, suggesting that boys were at higher risk for exhibiting cyberbullying. School-bullying and cyberbullying at Year 1 predicted cyberbullying one year later. MVE and CU traits were each positively related to changes in cyberbullying above and beyond the variables entered in steps 1 and 2. Furthermore, family social support was related to decreases in cyberbullying a year later after taking into account all the risk factors. No significant interactions were found.

Cyber-victimization. According to Table 2, boys and adolescents living in single-parent households were more likely to be cyber-victimized. Step 2 suggested that Time 1 cyber-victimization and school victimization were positively related to Year 2 cyber-victimization. MVE was the only risk factor that predicted changes in cyber-victimization, and family social support was the only environmental protective factor negatively related to cyber-victimization.

There were two significant two-way interactions, parental marital status × family social support and family × friend social support, predicting Year 2 cyber-victimization. Furthermore, there was a significant three-way interaction between parental marital status, family, and friend social support. As a result, the two-way interactions were conditional on the significant three-way interaction, and thus only the higher order three-way interaction needs to be interpreted (Aiken & West, 1991). The results of the three-way interaction suggested that the family by friend social support interaction was only significant for single-parent households ($\beta_{family} \times \beta_{friend} = 0.29$, $p < .05$), but not for intact households ($\beta_{family} \times \beta_{friend} = 0.03$, $p = .38$). The significant interaction is depicted in Figure 1. The high and low points in the graphs represent values of one standard deviation above and below the mean. According to the graph, family social support was associated with decreases in cyber-victimization at low levels of friend

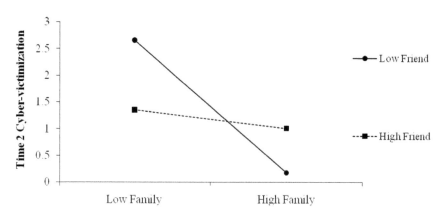

Figure 1. The interaction between Time 1 family and friend social support predicting Time 2 cyber-victimization (single-parent households).

social support ($\beta = -0.40$, $p < .01$), but not for high levels of friend social support ($\beta = -0.17$, $p = .29$). Thus, the stronger relation between family social support and cyber-victimization was obtained for adolescents living in single-parent households who reported the lowest levels of friend social support. This finding further suggests that at higher levels of family support, low friend support was not as detrimental for the development of cyber-victimization. In addition, low family support coupled with low friend support predicted the highest levels of cyber-victimization.

DISCUSSION

The current study contributes several novel findings to the literature investigating the development of cyberbullying and cyber-victimization during adolescence. Building on the ecological model of development the findings suggested that both individual and contextual predictors are important for the development of cyberbullying and cyber-victimization. Furthermore, cross-sectional and longitudinal associations between school-bullying and cyberbullying and between school-victimization and cyber-victimization were identified. Regarding gender differences, the results supported prior research in that boys reported higher incident rates of cyberbullying (e.g., Li, 2007), although is inconsistent with prior studies suggesting that girls are more vulnerable to be cyber-victimized (Calvete et al., 2010). Actually, compared to girls, boys in our sample were at higher risk for all forms of bullying and victimization, to be characterized by psychopathic traits, to be exposed to media violence and to perceive lower friend social support.

On the individual level, the findings provided evidence for the importance of CU traits as a risk factor for the involvement of adolescents in cyberbullying. Prior research has suggested that CU traits constitute an important predictor of school-bullying behaviour and that they characterize bullies but not victims of bullying behaviour (Fanti et al., 2009). The current findings extend this line of work in that CU traits have the power to differentiate bullies from victims within different contexts, school and technology. Compared to youth scoring low on CU traits, youth high on CU traits tend to recognize poorly and pay less attention to others' distress cues, and they lack concern for others' feelings (Kimonis, Frick, Fazekas, & Loney, 2006; Pardini, Lochman, & Frick, 2003). Thus, the fear and distress experienced by victims of cyberbullying may be less inhibitory for adolescents scoring high on CU traits. They are also more likely to expect that aggression will result in positive outcomes (e.g., peer dominance; Pardini et al., 2003), which is possibly one factor leading to the continuation of this type of behaviour.

An additional risk factor leading to the development of both cyberbullying and cyber-victimization was MVE. It is possible that MVE may lead to different interpretations of the witnessed aggressive action (Berkowitz, 1984). Cyberbullies might perceive the aggressive behaviour they view as appropriate, profitable, or even morally justified, which is likely to increase their own aggressive behaviour. Repeated exposure to media violence has also been shown to desensitize viewers to media violence, and as a result viewers may feel less sympathetic toward the victims of violence (Fanti et al., 2009). However, cyber-victims exposed to media violence might perceive the world as mean and scary, which will possibly lead to an increased fear and higher vulnerability of being victimized be peers. Reducing MVE (TV, videotape, and video games) has been shown to result in the reduction of aggressive behaviour and reductions in the perceptions that the world is mean and scary (Robinson, Wilde, Navracruz, Haydel, & Varady, 2001).

Finally, within the framework of the ecological perspective, the findings of this study, consistent with prior research (e.g., Wang et al., 2009), highlight the potential role of parents in protecting youth from engaging in both cyberbullying and cyber-victimization. Adolescents reporting greater family support reported fewer incidents of cyberbullying and cyber-victimization a year later. While examining the interaction between the different sources of social support, it was found that among children living in single-parent households, perceived family social support was associated with decreases in cyber-victimization at low levels of friend social support. Thus, feeling supported by family may protect adolescents from cyber-victimization when their friendships are not supportive. Furthermore, adolescents living in single-parent homes who were exposed to low family and low friend social support were at greater risk for being cyber-victimized in the future. As a result, the interrelated social networks of friends and family members are important for protecting youth from being cyber-victimized, agreeing with prior work suggesting that a child is more likely to be victimized when he or she is interpersonally at risk (Hodges & Perry, 1999). This association is especially important among children from single-parent families who, compared to children from intact families, were more likely to be cyber-victimized by their peers.

Strengths, limitations, and conclusions

The large sample of early adolescents, which allowed for testing and interpreting interactions, and the short-term longitudinal design were strengths of this investigation. However, additional time points of measurement would have allowed for the investigation of trajectories of change over time. Moreover, data were based solely on adolescent self-report for all variables, and the correlations among them could have been inflated due to shared method variance. Nevertheless, the validity of self-report measures on behavioural problems and personality increases during the adolescence age period and self-report instruments administered to adolescents have the advantage of measuring individual attitudes and emotions that may not be apparent to other people (Essau, Sasagawa, & Frick, 2006; Kamphaus & Frick, 1996).

In conclusion, our findings provide evidence that in order to understand the development of cyberbullying and cyber-victimization it is important to consider both individual traits and contextual variables. The current study replicates prior work showing that MVE, family social support, and school forms of bullying and victimization are associated with cyberbullying and cyber-victimization. The findings further suggest that psychopathic traits, and more specifically CU traits, predict the development of cyberbullying, supporting the need for further research in this area. By controlling for initial levels of cyberbullying and cyber-victimization, we also provide evidence that CU traits, MVE, and family social support influence the development of this new form of bullying and victimization. Identifying risk and protective factors related to both cyberbullying and cyber-victimization is important for the design of new preventive interventions.

REFERENCES

Aiken, L. S., & West, S. G. (1991). *Multiple regression: Testing and interpreting interactions.* Newbury Park, CA: Sage.

Ang, R. P., Ong, E., Lim, J., & Lim, E. W. (2010). From narcissistic exploitativeness to bullying behavior: The mediating role of approval-of-aggression beliefs. *Social Development, 19,* 721–735.

Beran, T., & Li, Q. (2005). Cyber-harassment: A study of a new method for an old behavior. *Journal of Educational Computing Research, 32,* 265–277.

Berkowitz, L. (1984). Some effects of thoughts on anti- and prosocial influences of media events: A cognitive neoassociation analysis. *Psychological Bulletin, 95,* 410–427.

Bronfenbrenner, U. (1979). *The ecology of human development: Experiments by nature and design.* Cambridge, MA: Harvard University Press.

Brookmeyer, K. A., Fanti, K. A., & Henrich, C. C. (2006). Schools, parents, and youth violence: A multilevel, ecological analysis. *Journal of Clinical Child and Adolescent Psychology, 35,* 504–514.

Calvete, E., Orue, I., Estévez, A., Villardón, L., & Padilla, P. (2010). Cyberbullying in adolescences: Modalities and aggressors' profile. *Computers in Human Behavior, 26,* 1128–1135.

Canty-Mitchell, J., & Zimet, G. D. (2000). Psychometric properties of the multidimensional scale of perceived social support in urban adolescents. *American Journal of Community Psychology, 28,* 391–399.

Eliot, M., Cornell, D., Gregory, A., & Fa, X. (2010). Supportive school climate and student willingness to seek help for bullying and threats of violence. *Journal of School Psychology, 48,* 533–553.

Essau, C. A., Sasagawa, S., & Frick, P. J. (2006). Callous-unemotional traits in community sample of adolescents. *Assessment, 13,* 454–469.

Fanti, K. A., Frick, P. J., & Georgiou, S. (2009). Linking callous-unemotional traits to instrumental and non-instrumental forms of aggression. *Journal of Psychopathology and Behavioral Assessment, 31*, 285–298.

Fanti, K. A., Vanman, E., Henrich, C. C., & Avraamides, M. N. (2009). Desensitization to media violence over a short period of time. *Aggressive Behavior, 35*, 179–187.

Finn, J. (2004). A survey of online harassment at a university campus. *Journal of Interpersonal Violence, 19*, 468–483.

Frick, P. J. (2004). *The Inventory of Callous-Unemotional Traits.* Unpublished rating scale. University of New Orleans.

Frick, P. J., & Dickens, C. (2006). Current perspective on conduct disorder. *Current Psychiatry Reports, 8*, 59–72.

Frick, P. J., & Hare, R. D. (2001). *The Antisocial Process Screening Device.* Toronto, Canada: Multi-Health Systems.

Frick, P. J., & White, S. F. (2008). The importance of callous-unemotional traits for the development of aggressive and antisocial behavior. *Journal of Child Psychology and Psychiatry, 49*, 359–375.

Funk, J. B., Bechtoldt-Baldacci, H., Pasold, T., & Baumgartner, J. (2004). Violence exposure in real-life, video games, television, movies, and the internet: Is there desensitization? *Journal of Adolescence, 27*, 23–39.

Griffin, K. W., Botvin, G. J., Scheier, L. M., Diaz, T., & Miller, N. L. (2000). Parenting practices as predictors of substance use, delinquency, and aggression among urban minority youth. *Psychology of Addictive Behaviors, 14*, 174–184.

Hodges, E. V., & Perry, D. G. (1999). Personal and interpersonal antecedents and consequences of victimization by peers. *Journal of Personality and Social Psychology, 76*, 677–685.

Hunt, M. H., Meyers, J., Jarrett, O., & Neel, J. (2005). *Student survey of bullying behavior: Preliminary development and results from six elementary schools.* Atlanta, GA: Georgia State University, Center for Research on School Safety, School Climate and Classroom Management.

Juvonen, J., & Gross, F. E. (2008). Extending the school grounds? Bullying experiences in cyberspace. *Journal of School Health, 78*, 496–505.

Kamphaus, R. W., & Frick, P. J. (1996). *Clinical assessment of child and adolescent personality and behavior.* Needham Heights, MA: Allyn & Bacon.

Kimonis, E. R., Frick, P. J., Fazekas, H., & Loney, B. R. (2006). Psychopathy, aggression, and the processing of emotional stimuli in non-referred girls and boys. *Behavioral Sciences & the Law. 24*, 21–37.

Kimonis, E. R., Frick, P. J., Skeem, J., Marsee, M. A., Cruise, K., Munoz, L. C., Aucoin, K. J., & Morris, A. S. (2008). Assessing callous-unemotional traits in adolescent offenders: Validation of the Inventory of Callous-Unemotional Traits. *Journal of the International Association of Psychiatry and Law, 31*, 241–252.

Kuntsche, E., Pickett, W., Overpeck, M., Craig, W., Boyce, W., & Gaspar de Matos, M. (2006). Television viewing and forms of bullying among adolescents from eight countries. *Journal of Adolescent Health, 39*, 908–915.

Li, Q. (2007). New bottle but old wine: A research of cyberbullying in schools. *Computers in Human Behavior, 23*, 1777–1791.

McCullough, M. E., Emmons, R. A., Kilpatrick, S. D., & Mooney, C. N. (2003). Narcissists as "victims": The role of narcissism in the perception of transgressions. *Personality and Social Psychology Bulletin, 29*, 885–893.

Munoz, L. C., & Frick, P. J. (2007). The reliability, stability, and predictive utility of the self-report version of the Antisocial Process Screening Device. *Scandinavian Journal of Psychology, 48*, 299–312.

O'Brennan, L. M., Bradshaw, C. P., & Sawyer, A. L. (2009). Examining development differences in the social-emotional problems among frequent bullies, victims, and bully/victims. *Psychology in the Schools, 46,* 100–115.

Olweus, D. (1993). *Bullying at school.* Oxford, UK: Blackwell Publishers.

Olweus, D. (1995). Bullying or peer abuse at school: Facts and interventions. *Current Directions in Psychological Science, 4,* 196–200.

Pardini, D. A., Lochman, J. E., & Frick, P. J. (2003). Callous/unemotional traits and social-cognitive processes in adjudicated youths. *Journal of the American Academy of Child & Adolescent Psychiatry, 42,* 364–371.

Patchin, J. W., & Hinduja, S. (2006). Bullies move beyond the schoolyard: A preliminary look at cyberbullying. *Youth Violence Juvenile Justice, 4,* 148–169.

Pellegrini, A. D., & Bartini, M. (2000). A longitudinal study of bullying, victimization, and peer affiliation during the transition from primary school to middle school. *American Educational Research Journal, 37,* 669–725.

Robinson, T., Wilde, M., Navracruz, L., Haydel, K. F., & Varady, A. (2001). Effects of reducing children's television and video game use on aggressive behavior. *Pediatric Adolescent Medicine, 155,* 17–23.

Smith, P. K., Mahdavi, J., Carvalho, M., Fisher, S., Russell, S., & Tippett, N. (2008). Cyberbullying: Its nature and impact in secondary school pupils. *Journal of Child Psychology and Psychiatry, 49,* 376–385.

Sroufe, L. A., & Rutter, M. (1984). The domain of developmental psychopathology. *Child Development, 55,* 17–29.

Strom, P. S., & Strom, R. D. (2005). When teens turn cyberbullies. *The Educational Digest, 71,* 35–41.

Swartz, M. K. (2009). Cyberbullying: An extension of the schoolyard. *Journal of Pediatric Health Care, 23,* 281–282.

Turner, H. A., Finkelhor, D., & Ormrod, R. (2007). Family structure variations in patterns and predictors of child victimization. *American Journal of Orthopsychiatry, 77,* 282–295.

Varjas, K., Meyers, J., & Hunt, M. H. (2006). *Student Survey of Bullying Behavior – Revised 2 (SSBB-R2).* Atlanta, GA: Georgia State University, Center for Research on School Safety, School Climate and Classroom Management.

Wang, J., Iannotti, R. J., & Nansel, T. R. (2009). School-bullying among adolescents in the United States: Physical, verbal, relational, and cyber. *Journal of Adolescent Health, 45,* 368–375.

Williams, K. R., & Guerra, N. G. (2007). Prevalence and predictors of internet bullying. *Journal of Adolescence Health, 41,* 14–21.

Zimet, G. D., Dahlem, N. W., Zimet, S. G., & Farley, G. K. (1988). The multidimensional scale of perceived social support. *Journal of Personality Assessment, 52,* 30–41.

Zimmerman, F. J., Glew, G. M., Christakis, D. A., & Katon, W. (2005). Early cognitive stimulation, emotional support and television watching as predictors of bullying among grade-school children. *Archives of Pediatric Adolescent Medicine, 159,* 384–388.

Recalling unpresented hostile words: False memories predictors of traditional and cyberbullying

Manila Vannucci[1], Annalaura Nocentini[1], Giuliana Mazzoni[2], and Ersilia Menesini[1]

[1]Department of Psychology, University of Florence, Florence, Italy
[2]Department of Psychology, University of Hull, Hull, UK

This study investigated the relationship between hostile false memories (violent and verbal/aggressive) and engagement in traditional and cyberbullying, controlling for their co-occurrence. Two hundred eleven adolescents completed measures of traditional and cyberbullying and performed a modified version of the "DRM paradigm", a false memory task for lists of associated words. Five lists were used: one of ambiguously violent words, one of insults and three lists of neutral words used as controls. For each list a free recall task was performed. A path analysis showed that both violent false memories for ambiguously hostile words and verbal/aggressive false memories for insults were positively associated with cyberbullying and, in males, also with traditional bullying. These data indicate a contribution of hostile memory distortions to bullying behaviours in adolescents. Findings are discussed according to the general aggression model.

Keywords: False memories; Bullying; Cyberbullying; Aggression.

INTRODUCTION

The main purpose of the present study was to examine the relationship between hostile (violent and verbal/aggressive) false memories and

Correspondence should be addressed to Manila Vannucci, Department of Psychology, Via San Salvi 12, Padiglione 26, Florence, Italy. E-mail: manila.vannucci@psico.unifi.it

The current research was co-funded by the Italian Ministry of University and Research (PRIN 2007).

The authors would like to thank Alessandro Vittori, Andrea Beretta and Benedetta Palladino for their help with data collection.

engagement in traditional and cyberbullying in a group of adolescents, controlling for their co-occurrence.

In current models of aggressive behaviour, the role of cognitive and memory factors in learning and maintaining aggressive behaviour is central. According to the general aggression model (GAM; Anderson & Bushman, 2002), aggression is mainly based on the learning, activation and application of aggression-related knowledge structures (e.g., schemas and scripts) stored in memory. The GAM posits that these cognitions derive from both personal (e.g., traits, values) and situational factors (e.g., provocation, exposure to aggressive cues) that would increase, either chronically or temporarily, the accessibility of aggressive knowledge structures in memory and would make them more familiar (Anderson & Bushman, 2002). The activation of these schemas would therefore mediate aggressive behaviour, "filtering" current perceptions and interpretations of the social environment and making people more likely to expect hostility and aggression in future interactions and to choose to react aggressively, thereby fuelling an escalating cycle.

Most of the research on aggressive cognitions has focused on a specific kind of aggressive scripts, the hostile biases, which take several forms, including the tendency to perceive and interpret ambiguous acts by others in a relatively hostile way, to perceive aggression as common in interactions among others, and to expect that many social interactions will be characterized by hostility and aggression (see Orobio de Castro, Veerman, Koops, Bosch, & Monshouwer, 2002, for a review). Hostile biases have been consistently reported both in aggressive individuals (Crick & Dodge, 1994; Dill, Anderson, Anderson, & Deuser, 1997) and in non-aggressive individuals induced into an aggressive state (e.g., Anderson & Bushman, 2001).

A recent study by Takarangi, Polaschek, Hignett, and Garry (2008) has gone a step further in investigating aggression-related cognitions, showing that when chronically or temporally aggressive people encounter ambiguously hostile information, they not only remember the information in a hostile way, they also create completely false hostile memories, remembering additional hostile and yet completely false information. The authors employed a modified and shortened version of the classical Deese–Roediger–McDermott (DRM) paradigm for associated words (Deese, 1959; Roediger & McDermott, 1995). In this task, participants study lists of words. In each list words are associated with a non-studied but semantically related lure (e.g., *bed, rest, awake* ... all associated with *sleep*), which is falsely recalled with relatively high probability. In the study, introductory psychology students with high and low scores on a measure of aggressive personality were asked to recall three lists of neutral semantically related words and an ambiguous list comprised of homonyms that could be interpreted as having a violent or a kitchen theme (e.g., *cut, whip, mug, knife, beat* ...). Half of the participants were primed with a list of insult words that they had to read and recall before performing the memory task with the ambiguous list. The results showed that both trait aggression and priming with insult words increased the likelihood of falsely recalling non-presented, clearly violent words in the ambiguous list.

Such false recall of violent words in these participants might be explained as due to the activation of the conceptual node of violence, or a "violent" gist, resulting in other violent words coming to mind. In line with the GAM, hostile memory distortions may strongly affect the way information and others' behaviour are processed, reinforcing and consolidating aggressive-distorted cognitive schemas and, therefore, the subsequent behaviour towards other people.

To date, no studies have investigated the production of aggression-related false memories in relation to a specific subcategory of aggressive behaviour, that is, bullying. Bullying is a subcategory of aggression that is intentionally carried out by one or more individuals and repeatedly targeted towards a person who cannot easily defend him/herself (Olweus, 1993). Imbalance of power and repetition distinguish aggression from bullying. Bullying usually occurs within social relationships and in the presence of peers. It may take different forms (direct and indirect) and seems to be highly related to status acquisition (e.g., Salmivalli, 2010). In relation to aggression-related cognitions, studies have found that bullies expect positive outcomes from their bullying behaviour, and they perform aggression because they expect it helps reach their aims (e.g., Sutton, Smith, & Swettenham, 1999). On the contrary, mixed results have been found for the presence of hostile attribution biases (Camodeca & Goossens, 2005; Gini, 2006).

Recently, the advent of widespread use of electronic media has given rise to a new form of bullying, referred to as cyberbullying. It is defined as "an aggressive, intentional act carried out by a group or individual repeatedly and over time using electronic media against a victim who cannot easily defend him or herself" (Smith et al., 2008). A large amount of cyberbullying is text/verbal-based (e.g., teasing, insulting, harassing and threatening by phone calls, text messages and e-mails), but it also includes online social exclusion, defaming websites and compromising photos or videos circulating on mobile phones and on the internet.

Relatively little is still known about various aspects of cyberbullying, including similarities and differences with traditional face-to-face bullying. If it is true that in many cases cyberbullies are also involved in traditional bullying, and cyberbullying represents an extension of traditional bullying (Gradinger, Strohmeier, & Spiel, 2009; Ybarra & Mitchell, 2004), there are also adolescents who engage in cyberbullying only. For these cases, considering cyberbullying as merely the electronic version of the traditional bullying may underestimate the specificity of the two behaviours. For example the reward for engaging in cyberbullying is often delayed compared to traditional bullying (Dooley, Pyzalski, & Cross, 2009), and this may have an effect on how goals for these aggressive acts are formed and pursued. The anonymous feature is also an important characteristic of cyberbullying, as well as the public and intrusive nature of the cyber-attack that might easily reach a wide audience and target the victims at any time and in any place (Dooley et al., 2009).

To date, no research has compared cognitive correlates of traditional and cyberbullying. The only study (Pornari & Wood, 2010) that examined aggression-related cognitions, namely hostile attribution bias and positive outcomes expectancies, compared traditional peer and cyber-aggression and victimization among school children. In this study positive outcome expectancies were found to be a positive predictor of traditional but not of cyber-aggression, and hostile attribution was negatively correlated with traditional but not with cyber-aggression. However, the authors measured traditional and cyber-aggression and not bullying, and the co-occurrence of the two types of peer-aggression was not controlled.

In the present study, we aimed to investigate the relationship between aggression-related memory distortions and bullying behaviour in adolescents and to verify whether traditional and cyberbullying are associated with similar or different patterns of memory distortion. Given the high incidence of verbal attacks in bullying (Rigby, 1997), we investigated not only false memories for ambiguously hostile material, but also false memories for verbal/aggressive material, namely lists of offensive words as insults and offences. We hypothesize that both forms of bullying are likely to lead to false violent memories when people are presented with a list of ambiguously violent words. We also hypothesized that bullies are likely to create false memories for offensive words, as insults. Finally, given the more indirect and symbolic nature of cyber-bullying, it can be also hypothesized that it is more strongly associated with false memories for offensive words, compared with traditional bullying.

To analyse the contribution of violent and verbal/aggressive false memories for cyberbullying and traditional bullying, controlling for their co-occurrence, we conducted a path analysis using a multiple-group approach to test for gender differences. Gender is a relevant variable in studies of aggression and bullying. Overall, males are associated with a higher risk for traditional bullying (Olweus, 1993; Boulton & Smith, 1994). For cyberbullying, results are more complex. While it is accepted that females report being victimized more often than males, mixed results have been obtained for cyberbullying perpetration. For instance, males presented higher levels of bullying through text messages, photos or video clips of intimate scenes, and insults on websites and in chatrooms, while for other behaviours no differences were found (Menesini, Calussi, & Nocentini, 2012). Given the relevance of this variable, the path analysis evaluates whether the hypothesized associations are similar or different across gender.

Finally, to control for a more general tendency to create false memories in our participants, in addition to the list of ambiguously hostile words and the list of insult words, the three lists of semantically related neutral words used in Takarangi et al. (2008) were added.

METHODS

Participants

A sample of 211 adolescents, 66 males (31.3%) and 145 females (68.7%), enrolled in 9th to 13th grades of eight high schools in Tuscany (Italy), participated in the study. The age of participants ranged between 14 and 20 years, with an average age of 15.9 years ($SD = 1.33$ years). The choice of the sample was mainly related to the developmental trend of cyberbullying, which seems to be more frequent in adolescents than in school children and pre-adolescents (Smith et al., 2008).

All were native Italian speakers with normal or corrected-to-normal hearing. Of the students, 80% attended Social Lyceum high schools, while 20% attended Technical Institutes. Consent procedure for research consisted of approval by the schools and consent provided by the parents. Due to the prolonged collaboration with these school districts, 100% of the families agreed to their children's participation in the research.

Measures and materials

Cyberbullying. The Cyberbullying Scale (CS; Menesini, Nocentini, & Calussi, 2011) was used. After a general definition of cyberbullying (Smith et al., 2008), we presented a multiple-item scale consisting of 10 items, asking about the frequency with which adolescents had perpetrated several behaviours in the past two months (i.e., nasty text messages, phone and internet pictures/photos or video clips of violent or intimate scenes, nasty or rude e-mails, insults in chatrooms). The frequency of each item was rated on a 5-point scale from 1 (*never*) to 5 (*several times a week*). The reliability coefficient of the scale was adequate ($\alpha = .67$). A mean score was used in the path analyses.

Bullying. Traditional bullying was measured with a scale in which participants were given a definition of bullying and were asked to rate on a 5-point scale, ranging from 1 (*never*) to 5 (*several times a week*), how often they had perpetrated each of 11 behaviours in the past two months (Menesini, Calussi et al., 2012). The scale included different types of behaviours: physical (physically hurt), verbal (i.e., teasing, name calling about ethnicity, about disability, about religion), indirect or psychological (leaving out, spreading rumours, threatening) and destruction or theft of property. A previous work (Menesini, Calussi et al., 2012) confirmed the monofactorial structure of this scale. The reliability coefficient showed an acceptable value ($\alpha = .80$). A mean score index was used.

DRM paradigm. Five lists of 12 semantically associated words were presented, including three lists of semantically associated neutral words (List 1, List 2, List 3, e.g., List 1 (*window*): *door, glass, pane, shade, ledge, sill, house, open* ...); one list of ambiguous words (List 4); and one list of insult words (List 5). The neutral lists were chosen from DRM lists (Roediger & McDermott, 1995, Experiment 1); the ambiguous list (homonyms that could be interpreted as having both a violent and a kitchen theme) was the same as in Takarangi et al. (2008) with some adaptations to the Italian language (*cut, whip, knife, beat, mortar, shake, burn, drown, butcher*) to which three words were added (*grind, flame, incision*) to have the same number of words in all lists. The three additional words were selected (as in Takarangi et al., 2008) by asking three colleagues to list some ambiguous words that could be interpreted as having both a violent and a kitchen theme. The insult list was a modification of the 9-word list developed by Takarangi et al. (2008) as a priming condition for one group of participants. Three additional words were added to the list (*idiot, loser, incapable, slob, fake, buffoon, pathetic, stupid, cheat, failure, liar, inept*). The new words were selected by asking three colleagues to list their top 10 insults and the three words indicated by them all were included.

Procedure

Participants were tested in two half-hour sessions scheduled two weeks apart. In Session 1, the self-report scales on traditional and cyberbullying were administered in class during school time by trained researchers. During Session 2, participants performed the DRM paradigm, in small groups. Subjects were instructed that they would hear lists of words to memorize, and would be tested after each list. At test, they had to write the words of each list on a separate page in a notebook provided by the experimenter. They were asked to write down words they were reasonably sure had been presented on the list and that they should not guess. The 12 words in each list were read aloud by the first author at the approximate rate of one word every 1.5 s. At the end of each list, subjects spent one minute working on math problems, then two minutes recalling words from the list in any order.

All subjects started with the neutral lists (List 1, List 2, List 3) followed by the ambiguous (List 4) and insult lists (List 5).

RESULTS

The aim of the study was to assess the production of violent and verbal/aggressive false memories. Hence, analyses were carried out primarily on number of violent intrusions recalled in the ambiguous list (List 4), False Recall_violent (FR_Violent), and number of verbal/aggressive intrusions recalled in the insult list (List 5), False Recall_insult (FR_Insult).

As in Takarangi et al. (2008), violent intrusions were identified by presenting a list with the words falsely recalled by all participants to 10 independent judges (blind to conditions). Judges were asked to classify each word as having a kitchen, an ambiguous or a violent theme. The words rated as violent by at least 9 out of 10 judges were selected as violent words.

Although our focus was on violent and verbal/aggressive false memories, we also examined the total number of false recalls for the standard lists of neutral words (FR_Neutral) as a control. Descriptive data on these measures (FR_Neutral; FR_Violent; FR_Insult) and correlations between these measures and traditional and cyberbullying are reported in Table 1, separately for gender. No significant correlations were found between measures of bullying and false recalls for the standard lists of words (FR_Neutral). Traditional bullying was significantly correlated with both FR_Violent and FR_Insult in males, and cyberbullying was correlated with both FR_Violent and FR_Insult in both males and females. Moreover, in males, both FR_Violent and FR_Insult correlated with FR_neutral, while in females the pattern occurred only for FR_violent. Traditional and

TABLE 1
Descriptive data and correlations for males and females

	1	2	3	4	5	Mean (SD)
1. Cyberbullying	1	.62***	.10	.19**	.23**	1.05 (0.08)
2. Traditional bullying	.65***	1	.11	.23**	.25**	1.28 (0.24)
3. FR_Neutral	.13	.00	1	.37**	.32**	3.24 (2.17)
4. FR_Violent	.26**	.08	.25**	1	.30**	0.47 (0.80)
5. FR_Insult	.24**	.05	.10	.14	1	1.55 (1.22)
Mean (SD)	1.05 (0.09)	1.15 (0.16)	3.11 (2.18)	0.38 (0.66)	2.04 (1.67)	

Notes: ***$p < .001$; **$p < .01$; *$p < .05$. Males are above and females are below the diagonal. FR_Neutral = total number of false recalls for the standard lists of neutral words (Lists 1, 2, 3); FR_Violent = number of violent intrusions recalled in the ambiguous list (List 4); FR_Insult = number of verbal/aggressive intrusions recalled in the insult list (List 5).

cyberbullying were highly correlated, supporting the need to control for their co-occurrence.

The second analysis (path analysis) then tested the association between violent (FR_Violent), insult (verbal aggressive; FR_Insult) false memories, cyberbullying and traditional bullying, controlling for their co-occurrence. The path analysis used a multiple-group approach to test for gender differences as well.

The following steps were conducted: (1) *unconstrained multiple-group model* across gender, in which the same pattern of structural paths was tested without constraints across groups; and (2) *constrained multiple-group model*, where structural paths were constrained to be equal across groups. The analyses were conducted with MPlus version 4.2 (Muthen & Muthen, 2006) using maximum likelihood estimation. Referring to the asymmetrical distribution of the traditional and cyberbullying data, MLR estimator was used (maximum likelihood parameter estimates with standard errors and a chi-square test statistic that are robust to non-normality). Model fit was evaluated using the chi-square statistics, the root mean square error of approximation (*RMSEA*) and the comparative fit index (*CFI*). Recommended cut-off points for these measures are .06 for *RMSEA* and 0.95 for *CFI* (Hu & Bentler, 1998). In addition to these overall fit indices, the comparison between two nested models was tested through the significance of difference in the chi-square value. Using MLR estimator, the Satorra–Bentler scaled (mean-adjusted) chi-square was used for this purpose.

The chi-square of the baseline model (unconstrained) is 0, because it is a saturated model. The chi-square difference between the unconstrained and full constrained model was significant, $\Delta\chi^2(6) = 61.02$; $p = .000$, suggesting that one or more structural paths are different across gender. Looking at modification indices, we freed the beta from FR_Violent to traditional bullying across gender: the chi-square difference between the unconstrained and this partial constrained model was still significant, $\Delta\chi^2(5) = 17.48$; $p = .001$. Finally, we freed the beta from FR_Insult to traditional bullying across gender: the chi-square difference between the unconstrained and this partial constrained model was non-significant, $\Delta\chi^2(4) = 6.136$; $p = .19$, suggesting that this model can be accepted. The final fit indices of this model were: $\chi^2(4) = 1.930$; $p = .75$; scaling correction $= 1.258$; $CFI = 1.00$; $RMSEA = .000$.

Figure 1 shows the final standardized estimates for the partial constrained model across gender.

The model shows that, considering the consistent covariance of traditional and cyberbullying ($r = .33/.40$ for males and females, respectively) and the covariance between the two lists ($r = .22/.18$ for males and females, respectively), both FR_Violent list and FR_Insult list are significantly associated in males and females with cyberbullying, explaining

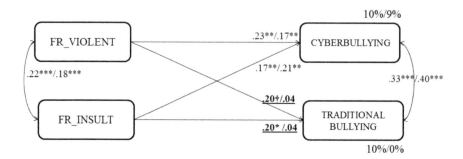

Fit indices: $\chi^2 (4) = 1.930$; $p = .75$; CFI = 1.00; RMSEA = .000

Figure 1. Multiple-group path analysis across gender: structural relations (standardized estimates) between False Recall Violent (FR_Violent) and False Recall Insult (FR_Insult) and the co-occurrence of traditional and cyberbullying. *Notes*: All the betas are invariant across gender. Values refer to males and females respectively. The underlined values are significantly different across gender. $^\dagger p = .08$; $*p < .05$; $**p < .01$; $***p < .001$.

around 10% and 9% of its variance respectively. These underlined paths are the same across gender. Furthermore, FR_Insult list and at a lower level FR_Violent list are significantly associated with traditional bullying in males, explaining around 10% of its variance. For females no significant paths from FR_Violent list and FR_Insult lists were found.

DISCUSSION

The main purpose of the present study was to examine the relationship between hostile (violent and verbal/aggressive) false memories and bullying behaviour in a group of adolescents, and to verify whether traditional and cyberbullying are associated with similar or different patterns of memory distortions.

Globally, our hypotheses have been confirmed. The patterns of correlations show that both violent false memories for ambiguous material and verbal/aggressive false memories for insults correlated positively with cyberbullying and, in males, also with traditional bullying. These results held also at the multivariate level, used to assess simultaneously the contribution of hostile and verbal aggressive memory predictors (controlling for their covariance) to both kinds of bullying behaviour in males and females. Thus, overall we can conclude that for males both types of false memories are associated with both types of bullying, but for females paths are significant only for cyberbullying. The lack of significant paths between false memories and traditional bullying in females can be mainly related to the rather uniformly low levels of this kind of bullying in girls.

Future studies on female bullying are needed in order to better understand these findings on gender differences as well as different types of attacks. There is consistency across the literature that for girls, indirect and social aggression are the main types of aggression expression (Björkqvist, Lagerspetz, & Kaukiainen, 1992). Our study used a global index of bullying, and this can underestimate girl bullying as compared to a more specific measure. Therefore, future studies should investigate more closely whether measuring social and indirect bullying, rather than using a global index of bullying behaviour, can lead to different results in females.

Overall the findings confirm and extend the results of a previous study carried out by Takarangi et al. (2008), indicating a specific contribution of hostile memory distortions for bullying behaviours. Given the cross-sectional nature of our study, direction of the relationship can go in both ways. On one hand, creating false hostile memories may enhance the likelihood of bullying and cyberbullying; on the other hand being involved in bullying and cyberbullying can activate learning processes and application of aggression-related knowledge in memory.

These findings and interpretation are consistent with current models of aggressive and bullying behaviour, in particular with both the general aggression model (GAM; Anderson & Bushman, 2002), and other social cognitive models of aggression (e.g., Crick & Dodge, 1994), which propose a crucial role of cognition and memory processes in learning and maintaining aggressive cognition and behaviour.

The paradigm we used to assess false memories, a modified version of the "DRM paradigm", makes it possible to identify the specific cognitive mechanisms underlying the relationship between aggressive cognitions and generation of hostile false memories. Two non-exclusive cognitive mechanisms, usually invoked to explain DRM false memories, can be advanced to explain why bullying is related to the creation of hostile and aggressive false memories. According to the first, the activation-monitoring approach (Roediger & McDermott, 1995), the role of activation is crucial. Hostile false memories are more likely to arise in bullies during the encoding of the lists of ambiguously hostile words and insult words due to the enhanced activation in memory of associated words and concepts, overtly violent in the case of the ambiguously hostile words, and verbal/aggressive, in the case of the insult words. This activation would make related intrusions more likely to be generated on a recall test, because the source of the activation is incorrectly monitored (or edited) and attributed to the actual presentation. A second mechanism stresses the role of extracting, during encoding, a hostile (violent or offensive) "gist" from the list of words (fuzzy-trace theory; see Reyna & Brainerd, 1995; Schacter, Norman, & Koutstaal, 1998). This makes related lures more familiar and therefore more likely to be confused with presented (familiar) words.

The fact that these mechanisms are more likely to occur in bullies and cyberbullies than in non-bullies, for both ambiguously violent words and insult words, suggests that, in bullies, violent/aggressive knowledge structures and concepts are easier to access than in non-aggressive adolescents. These concepts are easily extracted from associated verbal material, making bullies more vulnerable to the production of false memories for this information.

In the present study we also aimed to test for similarities and differences in memory distortions between traditional and cyberbullying. In particular our hypothesis that cyberbullying could be more strongly associated with false memories for offensive words was not supported by our data, and a similar pattern of memory distortions emerged for both kinds of bullying, at least for males. This is probably due to the fact that a verbal component is present and can play a relevant role (verbal forms in traditional and written-verbal forms in cyberbullying) in both phenomena, traditional and cyberbullying.

However, some limitations of the present study should be considered in the interpretation of these results. First, the instrument we used to measure cyberbullying did not allow us to distinguish between different forms of cyberbullying (written/verbal vs. visual) and to test the role of verbal forms and code on memory distortions. Similarly, the low number of physical acts characterizing our scale of traditional bullying did not allow us to verify the extent to which false memories for verbal aggressive material also characterize specific traditional forms of bullying and how they might be related to gender.

Our results also highlight the need for future large-scale studies, that make it possible to compare different groups of bullies, i.e., those who do not engage in bullying at all, those who only engage in traditional bullying, those who only engage in cyberbullying and those who do both. This would provide a more direct form of evidence of potential different cognitive mindsets associated with traditional and cyberbullying.

More research will also contribute to clarifying the complex relationship between cognitive processing, memory distortions and bullying behaviour. According to the GAM, repeated exposure to violence contributes to the development of aggression, making aggressive cognitions and memory chronically accessible and difficult to change. In the present study we focused on the relationship between aggression-related memories and behaviour, and we did not examine the role of exposure to violence. Future studies should include measures of familiarity with violence (i.e., a scale measuring familiar conflict or prolonged abuse from peers or other significant partners), to identify the dynamics underlying and consolidating bullying behaviour and clarify the role of memory distortions as predictors or mediators of behaviour. Finally, the cross-sectional design of this study cannot establish causality. Longitudinal and experimental study designs would help to address this issue.

In spite of these limitations, the study makes a relevant contribution to our understanding of bullying behaviour, demonstrating for the first time the presence of aggression-related memory distortions in adolescent bullies. As for potential implications, our study suggests that interventions or specific activities focusing on attributions and memory bias may have a role in tackling maladaptive/aggressive scripts and schemas.

REFERENCES

Anderson, C. A., & Bushman, B. J. (2001). Effects of violent video games on aggressive behavior, aggressive cognition, aggressive affect, physiological arousal, and prosocial behavior: A meta-analytic review of the scientific literature. *Psychological Science, 12*(5), 353–359.

Anderson, C. A., & Bushman, B. J. (2002). Human aggression. *Annual Review of Psychology, 53*, 27–51.

Björkqvist, K., Lagerspetz, K., & Kaukiainen, A. (1992). Do girls manipulate and boys fight? Developmental trends in regard to direct and indirect aggression. *Aggressive Behavior, 18*, 117–127.

Boulton, M. J., & Smith, P. K. (1994). Bully/victim problems in middle-school children: Stability, self-perceived competence, peer perceptions, and peer acceptance. *British Journal of Developmental Psychology, 12*, 315–329.

Camodeca, M., & Goossens, F. A. (2005). Aggression, social cognitions, anger and sadness in bullies and victims. *Journal of Child Psychology and Psychiatry, 46*(2), 186–197.

Crick, N. R., & Dodge, K. A. (1994). A review and reformulation of social information-processing mechanisms in children's social adjustment. *Psychological Bulletin, 115*(1), 74–101.

Deese, J. (1959). On the prediction of occurrence of particulate verbal intrusions in immediate recall. *Journal of Experimental Psychology, 58*, 17–22.

Dill, K. E., Anderson, C. A., Anderson, K. B., & Deuser, W. E. (1997). Effects of aggressive personality on social expectations and social perceptions. *Journal of Research in Personality, 31*, 272–292.

Dooley, J. J., Pyzalski, J., & Cross, D. (2009). Cyberbullying versus face-to-face bullying: A theoretical and conceptual review. *Zeitschrift für Psychologie/Journal of Psychology, 217*(4), 182–189.

Gini, G. (2006). Social cognition and moral cognition in bullying: What's wrong? *Aggressive Behavior, 32*(6), 528–539.

Gradinger, P., Strohmeier, D., & Spiel, C. (2009). Traditional bullying and cyberbullying: Identification of risks groups for adjustment problems. *Zeitschrift für Psychologie/Journal of Psychology, 217*(4), 205–213.

Hu, L., & Bentler, P. M. (1999). Cut-off criteria for fit indexes in covariance structure analysis: Conventional criteria versus new alternatives. *Structural Equation Modeling, 6*, 1–55.

Menesini, E., Calussi, P., & Nocentini, A. (2012). Cyberbullying and traditional bullying: Unique, addictive and synergistic effects on psychological health symptoms. In Q. Li, D. Cross, & P. Smith. (Eds.), *Cyberbullying in the global playground: Research from international perspectives* (pp. 245–262). Oxford, UK: Wiley-Blackwell.

Menesini, E., Nocentini, A., & Calussi, P. (2011). The measurement of cyberbullying: Dimensional structure and relative item severity and discrimination. *Cyberpsychology, Behavior and Social Networking, 14*(5), 267–274.

Muthen, L. K., & Muthen, B. O. (2006). *Mplus user's guide*. Los Angeles, CA: Author.

Olweus, D. (1993). *Bullying at school: What we know and what we can do*. Cambridge, MA: Blackwell.

Orobio de Castro, B., Veerman, J. W., Koops, W., Bosch, J. D., & Monshouwer, H. J. (2002). Hostile attribution of intent and aggressive behavior: A meta-analysis. *Child Development, 73*(3), 916–934.

Pornari, C. D., & Wood, J. (2010). Peer and cyber aggression in secondary school students: The role of moral disengagement, hostile attribution bias, and outcome expectancies. *Aggressive Behavior, 36*(2), 81–94.

Reyna, V. F., & Brainerd, C. J. (1995). Fuzzy-trace theory: An interim synthesis. *Learning and Individual Differences, 7*(1), 1–75.

Rigby, K. (1997). *Bullying in schools, and what to do about it*. London, UK: Jessica Kingsley.

Roediger, H. L., & McDermott, K. B. (1995). Creating false memories: Remembering words not presented in lists. *Journal of Experimental Psychology: Learning, Memory, and Cognition, 21*(4), 803–814.

Salmivalli, C. (2010). Bullying and the peer group: A review. *Aggression and Violent Behavior, 15*(2), 112–120.

Schacter, D. L., Norman, K. A., & Koutstaal, W. (1998). The cognitive neuroscience of constructive memory. *Annual Review of Psychology, 49*, 289–318.

Smith, P. K., Mahdavi, J., Carvalho, M., Fisher, S., Russell, S., & Tippett, N. (2008). Cyberbullying: Its nature and impact in secondary school pupils. *Journal of Child Psychology and Psychiatry, 49*(4), 376–385.

Sutton, J., Smith, P. K., & Swettenham, J. (1999). Bullying and "theory of mind": A critique of the "social skills deficit" view of antisocial behaviour. *Social Development, 8*(1), 117–127.

Takarangi, M. K. T., Polaschek, D. L. L., Hignett, A., & Garry, M. (2008). Chronic and temporary aggression causes hostile false memories for ambiguous information. *Applied Cognitive Psychology, 22*(1), 39–49.

Ybarra, M. L., & Mitchell, K. J. K. (2004). Youth engaging in online harassment: Associations with caregiver–child relationships, internet use, and personal characteristics. *Journal of Adolescence, 27*(3), 319–336.

Cyberbullying and traditional bullying in adolescence: Differential roles of moral disengagement, moral emotions, and moral values

Sonja Perren[1] and Eveline Gutzwiller-Helfenfinger[2]

[1]Jacobs Center for Productive Youth Development, University of Zürich, Zürich, Switzerland
[2]Department of Educational Research, University of Teacher Education, Lucerne, Switzerland

The aim of this study was to investigate whether different aspects of morality predict traditional bullying and cyberbullying behaviour in a similar way. Students between 12 and 19 years participated in an online study. They reported on the frequency of different traditional and cyberbullying behaviours and completed self-report measures on moral emotions and moral values. A scenario approach with open questions was used to assess morally disengaged justifications. Tobit regressions indicated that a lack of moral values and a lack of remorse predicted both traditional and cyberbullying behaviour. Traditional bullying was strongly predictive for cyberbullying. A lack of moral emotions and moral values predicted cyberbullying behaviour even when controlling for traditional bullying. Morally disengaged justifications were only predictive for traditional, but not for cyberbullying behaviour. The findings show that moral standards and moral affect are important to understand individual differences in engagement in both traditional and cyberforms of bullying.

Keywords: Bullying; Cyberbullying; Moral disengagement; Moral values; Moral emotions.

It has been repeatedly argued that bullies may have deficits regarding their morality (Hymel, Schonert-Reichl, Bonanno, Vaillancourt, & Henderson, 2010). Recent integrative models in developmental moral theory have

Correspondence should be addressed to Sonja Perren, Jacobs Center for Productive Youth Development, University of Zürich, Culmannstrasse 1, CH-8006 Zürich, Switzerland.
E-mail: perren@jacobscenter.uzh.ch

emphasized the need to investigate both moral cognition and moral affect in understanding individual differences in behaviours such as bullying (Arsenio & Lemerise, 2004; Malti & Latzko, 2010). We differentiate between two types of bullying: traditional bullying, including physical or verbal harassment, exclusion, relational aggression; and cyberbullying, involving the use of some kind of electronic media (i.e., internet or mobile phone) to engage in bullying behaviour. There is a significant conceptual and empirical overlap between both types of bullying (Dooley, Pyzalski, & Cross, 2009; Smith & Slonje, 2010). Nevertheless, it remains unclear whether similar psychological processes account for the occurrence of both types of bullying behaviour. The aim of the current study was to investigate the associations between both types of bullying and different indicators of morality in adolescents (morally disengaged justifications, feeling of remorse, and moral values).

Moral disengagement as a framework for understanding bullying

In the moral domain, Bandura's social cognitive theory of human agency offers an inclusive conceptual framework within which the moral dimensions of bullying can also be described. According to this framework, individuals' moral standards are used in a self-regulatory process to evaluate the potential consequences of intended behaviour for themselves. If—by violating their moral standards—self-condemnation (i.e., guilt) is antici-pated, the behaviour is not realized (Bandura, 2002). However, it is possible for individuals to enact behaviours that are not concordant with their moral standards without feeling guilty. To achieve this, individuals use cognitive mechanisms that can be selectively activated in order to escape negative self-evaluations and self-sanctions and thus allow them to morally disengage themselves from adherence to moral standards. According to this approach, moral values (standards), moral emotions, and moral justifications (cognitions) are important in understanding bullying behaviour.

Moral disengagement and bullying

A few studies in children and adolescents have used the conceptual framework of moral disengagement to investigate moral reasoning patterns among bullies. Several studies have shown that bullying is positively associated with self-reported moral disengagement in adolescents (Hymel, Rocke-Henderson, & Bonanno, 2005; Obermann, 2011) and in children (Gini, 2006; Gini, Pozzoli, & Hauser, 2011). A recent study by Pornari and Wood (2010) showed that moral disengagement is not only associated with traditional peer aggression but also with cyber aggression. A few studies have also used production measures to assess children's and adolescents' moral disengagement strategies and their associations with bullying.

34

Children and adolescents were asked to produce emotion attributions and justifications to a perpetrator in a hypothetical story. These studies showed that children (Perren, Gutzwiller-Helfenfinger, Groeben, Stadelmann, & von Klitzing, 2009) and adolescents (Perren, Gutzwiller-Helfenfinger, Malti, & Hymel, 2011) who were more frequently involved in bullying produced more morally disengaged and less morally responsible justifications. Bullies justified the moral transgression of a hypothetical bully mainly from an egocentric point of view, and their thinking centred on receiving personal benefit and profiting from their negative actions (Menesini et al., 2003).

Moral emotions and bullying

Moral emotions have been considered as mediators between moral standards and moral behaviour (see Tangney, Stuewig, & Mashek, 2007). They help children anticipate the negative outcomes of moral transgressions and enable them to adjust their moral behaviour accordingly (Malti, Gasser, & Buchmann, 2009).

Moral emotions have been intensively researched in the context of the happy victimizer paradigm. The "happy victimizer" describes a phenomenon in which there is a discrepancy between young children's understanding of moral rules and their attribution of positive emotions to perpetrators (Krettenauer, Malti, & Sokol, 2008). These studies showed significant associations between moral emotion attributions (i.e., emotions attributed to a perpetrator) and aggressive behaviour. A different line of research has investigated associations between moral emotions such as shame and guilt and their relation to moral behaviour (see Tangney et al., 2007).

Only a few studies have investigated the specific link between bullying and moral emotions. A study by Menesini and collaborators (2003) showed that bullies attributed pride and indifference to the perpetrator more frequently than did either victims or uninvolved children. A study by Ttofi and Farrington (2008) showed that positive shame management (i.e., a high level of acknowledgement of feelings of shame and remorse and a low level of shame displacement) was negatively associated with bullying. Likewise, Menesini and Camodeca (2008) reported negative associations between bullying and guilt and shame.

In sum, studies involving different methods and approaches have consistently indicated that bullying is associated with lower levels of moral emotions like guilt and shame and higher levels of emotions like pride or indifference in the context of moral transgressions, respectively.

Moral values and bullying

Besides moral emotions and moral disengagement strategies, the normative area (i.e., moral values, norms, standards, and beliefs) is also important to consider in attempts to explain the moral side of bullying. Moral standards are actively employed in exercising moral agency (Bandura, 2002; Blasi, 2001). However, moral values are not the only values individuals hold and adhere to. According to Schwartz (2006), individuals adapt their values to their life circumstances, upgrading the importance of those they can easily attain and downgrading the importance of those they cannot (easily) pursue.

Several studies have demonstrated a strong link between bullying behaviour and general pro-bullying or pro-aggression attitudes or norms (e.g., Salmivalli & Voeten, 2004). Laible, Eye, and Carlo (2008) identified the level of internalization of moral values as one aspect of moral cognition, which is negatively associated with bullying behaviour. However, our knowledge about these associations is rather limited, and we need research to assess the role of both endorsement and prioritizing of moral and other values in relation to bullying.

The specific role of morality in cyberbullying

As outlined above, morality is an important aspect to consider when explaining the occurrence of bullying behaviour. Most studies have investigated these associations in relation to traditional bullying. Only a few studies have investigated this link with respect to cyberbullying.

Although there is a high degree of empirical and conceptual overlap between traditional and cyberbullying, specific distinct features have been identified (Dooley et al., 2009; Smith et al., 2008). With respect to morality, the potential invisibility of the victim might be a specific feature of cyberbullying that is important to consider. Through the use of electronic forms of aggressive contact (cell phone, internet), there is an increased probability that the bully does not directly see the emotional impact of his/her actions on the victim. Because of this absence of direct contact it has been hypothesized that cyberbullying might make it easier for the bully both to act immorally without feeling guilty (Slonje & Smith, 2008) and to apply cognitive strategies to dissociate him/herself from moral responsibility (Almeida, Marinho, Esteves, Gomes, & Correia, 2008). However, as this applies also to indirect aggression (e.g., gossiping), the victims' invisibility may not be a specific feature of cyberbullying (Sticca & Perren, 2010). Nevertheless, the question emerges whether moral issues are more or less relevant to explain cyberbullying in comparison to traditional bullying. More specifically, we might ask whether there are differential effects of different indicators of morality (i.e., affect or cognitions) that are related to traditional forms or cyberforms of bullying, respectively.

On the other hand, it has been found that most cyberbullies also use more traditional forms of bullying (Raskauskas & Stoltz, 2007). Those "combined" bullies are bullying others with a larger repertoire of negative actions and maybe also bully more frequently (Perren & Sticca, 2011). Several studies have indicated that cyberbullies show more severe patterns of maladjustment than those who use only traditional forms (e.g., Gradinger, Strohmeier, & Spiel, 2009). Therefore, we might hypothesize that cyberbullies have stronger deficits in morality than bullies who engage in traditional forms only.

Research questions

Previous studies have suggested that bullying behaviour may be predicted by deficits in moral values, moral emotions (lack of remorse), and/or or morally disengaged justifications (cognitions). The aim of the current study was first to investigate whether those different indicators of morality predict traditional and cyberbullying in a similar way. We hypothesized significant positive associations between traditional bullying and cyberbullying (overlap) and significant associations between both types of bullying with higher moral disengagement, lower moral emotions, and lower moral values. As most cyberbullies also use traditional means of bullying, we also investigated whether morality specifically predicted cyberbullying when controlling for traditional bullying behaviour.

Due to developmental trends in bullying and morality we also investigated age differences. Traditional bullying decreases during adolescence, whereas cyberbullying increases over the years of secondary school (Smith & Slonje, 2010). Regarding morality, developmental trends indicate that children increasingly understand morally relevant situations like transgressions, judge them as wrong, and are able to anticipate the emotions of the persons involved (Krettenauer et al., 2008). However, only in older adolescence is morality fully integrated into the self, and individuals strive to maintain (personal) moral consistency and integrity (Blasi, 2001). Thus, we also investigated whether age moderates the associations between morality and bullying.

In addition, we analysed the role of gender. As far as gender differences are concerned, most studies agree that traditional bullying is more frequent in males (Stassen Berger, 2007), but results for cyberbullying are controversial (Smith & Slonje, 2010). Based on previous research, we also expected that females would show more moral emotions and less moral disengagement than males (Paciello, Fida, Tramontano, Lupinetti, & Caprara, 2008; Perren et al., 2011; Tangney et al., 2007). In addition to these main effects of gender, we also explored whether gender moderates the investigated associations.

METHOD

Procedure

A link to an online questionnaire (NetQ) was posted on a large social networking site for German-speaking students (*SchülerVZ*). SchülerVZ is accessible to students (who must be attending some sort of school) between 12 and 21 years of age. The link was placed online for three hours during one Wednesday afternoon (which is out of school hours) in November 2009. Thus, the sample represents a self-selected sample of students who were active users of this social networking site.

Before completing the questionnaire, students were informed about the goals of the study and gave their informed consent. As in anonymous online studies parental consent cannot be obtained, we decided to use a procedure approaching a "terms of use agreement". We informed participants that parental consent was necessary for this study and required participants under 18 years to click whether their parents agreed to their participation in this study. A similar procedure has been used by other studies (e.g., Hinduja & Patchin, 2008). Students who indicated that their parents did not consent to their participation in the study were not allowed to complete the questionnaire ($N = 174$). An automatic filter option directed them to a page informing them that they could not participate because their parents had not given permission.

In order to protect students' anonymity, only a few person variables were collected (gender, age). We assumed that risks associated with this anonymous online survey were very low. Participation was voluntary and participants were allowed to discontinue at any time or to skip any question. Participating students were offered an incentive of €5 (in the form of an electronic voucher for legal music download). To receive this voucher, they had to give an e-mail address. E-mail addresses were only used to send the voucher and were saved separately on a secured server. About 10% of participants actively withheld their contact details.

Participants

In total, 564 students partly or fully completed the questionnaire. Only adolescents (< 20 years) with complete data sets were included in the current paper ($N = 495$, 47% females). Participants' age was distributed fairly evenly between 12 and 19 years.

Assessment of traditional and cyberbullying

Participants reported on the *frequency of bullying* over the last three months ($1 = never$, $2 = once\ or\ twice$, $3 = once\ a\ month$, $4 = once\ a\ week$, $5 = almost$

every day). Six items covered traditional and five items cyberbullying behaviours, respectively. Items were introduced by providing a general definition of bullying, which included negative behaviours such as sending or spreading nasty messages or pictures. For the items we did not use the term cyberbullying but we relied on behavioural descriptions. Item order was completely randomized.

A principal component analysis with Varimax rotation including all eleven items yielded two distinct factors (eigenvalue > 1) for traditional and cyberbullying behaviour, respectively. Two items of the traditional bullying scale (threatening and destroying property) loaded equally on both factors and were excluded from the final bullying scales. Mean scores were computed. The *traditional bullying* scale encompassed four items (verbal aggression; physical aggression; exclusion; gossiping; $\alpha = .77$). The *cyberbullying* scale encompassed five items (sent nasty or threatening e-mails; nasty messages on the internet/to mobile phone; and mean or nasty comments or pictures sent to websites/other students' mobile phones; $\alpha = .89$).

To confirm the distinctiveness of the traditional and cyberbullying scale we also computed a confirmatory factor analysis (CFA) including those nine items with two latent factors. The CFA indicated an acceptable model fit: $\chi^2 = 84.7$ ($df = 21$); $CFI = .974$; $RMSEA = .073$ (Kline, 1998). The correlation between both latent factors was rather high: $r = .73$, $p < .001$.

Assessment of indicators of morality

Moral disengagement. This was assessed through a production measure (Perren et al., 2011). Participants were given two hypothetical aggression scenarios, both describing a student being hurt by another student. The first scenario described an adolescent intentionally misinforming another adolescent about a meeting with friends (exclusion scenario), and the second described an adolescent disseminating embarrassing pictures of a peer (humiliation scenario). Whether the perpetrator of the scenarios used cyber or traditional means for hurting (text message/internet vs. talking/ printed picture) was randomly assigned (Sticca & Perren, 2010). Both vignettes were followed by questions assessing participant's moral rule understanding (Q1: "Is it right to give wrong directions or not?" "Why?"); emotion attributions to hypothetical victimizer (Q2: "How does he/she feel?" "Why?"); moral evaluation of emotion attributions to hypothetical victimizer (Q3: "Is it right or not that he/she feels this way?" "Why?"); and moral evaluation regarding self as hypothetical perpetrator (Q4: "How would you feel?" "Why?"; see Malti et al., 2009). Moral justifications were established on the basis of students' written answers to the "why" questions.

Based on Menesini et al.'s (2003) conceptual model, we differentiated between morally responsible and disengaged justifications. For the current paper, only disengaged justifications referring to participants' own personal moral evaluations (Questions 1, 3, and 4) were used. Disengaged justifications included egocentric disengagement (e.g., hedonistic reasoning, euphemistic language, minimizing/distorting consequences); deviant rules (e.g., moral justifications, attributions of blame, advantageous comparisons, displacement or diffusion of responsibility); as well as dehumanization of the victim (see also Menesini et al., 2003).

Written answers were coded by two independent raters who were blind toward other data, 20% of interviews were coded by both. Inter-rater agreement was rather high (ICC, single measure = .827). Mean scores of all three questions across both scenarios were computed (6 questions; $\alpha = .62$).

Moral emotions (remorse). These were assessed through self-reports of feelings of remorse/guilt regarding 10 different (cyber)aggression scenarios ($\alpha = .93$): "If you had done this, would you have a guilty conscience?" (1 = *not at all* to 5 = *extremely*).

Moral values. These were assessed through a 6-item self-report measure ($\alpha = .77$). Students completed the Ideal Self Value Ratings (Campbell, 2004; Pratt, Hunsberger, Pancer, & Alisat, 2003). Students were asked to what extent they thought that each of a set of 12 values "should be important for them in their lives" (e.g., "Fair and just: Treat all people equally; don't put people down"). Six of these values were prototypically moral in nature (including trustworthy, good citizen, honest/truthful, kind and caring, fair and just, shows integrity), and could be used as a general index of commitment to a moral valuing self (Campbell, 2004).

RESULTS

Descriptive statistics and gender differences

As all scales were skewed, we used non-parametric tests for statistical analyses. Table 1 shows means and standard deviations of all variables divided by gender. A Kruskal–Wallis test showed significant gender differences regarding traditional bullying and all indicators of morality, but not regarding cyberbullying. Boys reported higher levels of bullying, lower levels of moral values, moral emotions (remorse), and produced more disengaged justifications.

Bivariate associations

To analyse bivariate associations, Spearman correlations were computed (Table 2). No significant associations emerged between age, morality, and bullying. Traditional and cyberbullying were positively correlated. Both types of bullying showed significant negative associations with moral values, moral emotions (remorse), and positive associations with disengaged justifications.

Multivariate analyses

In the following analyses, we accounted for the non-normality of the dependent variables through log transformations and the use of tobit regressions (Osgood, Finken, & McMorris, 2002).

TABLE 1
Descriptive results by gender

	Scale	Girls (N = 243) M (SD)	Boys (N = 252) M (SD)	Gender differences χ^2	p
Bullying					
Traditional bullying	1–5	1.61 (0.71)	1.85 (0.92)	8.12	.004
Cyberbullying	1–5	1.15 (0.47)	1.14 (0.44)	0.11	.741
Morality					
Disengaged justifications	0–1	0.07 (0.13)	0.16 (0.21)	33.8	<.001
Moral emotions (remorse)	1–5	3.94 (0.84)	3.44 (0.94)	38.8	<.001
Moral values	1–5	4.31 (0.61)	4.14 (0.66)	11.8	.001

Note: Non-parametric test: Kruskal–Wallis.

TABLE 2
Bivariate associations

	Traditional bullying	Cyberbullying	Justifications	Emotions	Moral values
Age	−.025	−.068	.051	.070	.039
Traditional bullying	–	.399**	.324**	−.402**	−.311**
Cyberbullying		–	.138**	−.320**	−.205**
Disengaged justifications			–	−.352**	−.306**
Moral emotions (remorse)				–	.475**
Moral values					–

Notes: Spearman correlations, two-tailed; **p < .01 (N = 495).

In a first set of analyses main effects of morality indicators were tested on (a) traditional bullying, (b) cyberbullying, and (c) on cyberbullying when controlling for traditional bullying. In a second set of analyses, age and gender interactions were included.

Morality predicting traditional bullying and cyberbullying. Tobit regressions indicated that low levels of moral values and of moral emotions and high levels of disengaged justifications predicted higher levels of traditional bullying. Low levels of moral values and moral emotions also predicted higher levels of cyberbullying; both effects remained significant when controlling for traditional bullying (see Table 3).

Age group and gender as moderators. In a second series of tobit regressions, we added age and gender as interaction effect. Age was included in the analysis as linear variable. The analysis yielded no significant interaction effects.

DISCUSSION

In agreement with other studies (Smith & Slonje, 2010), we found a high overlap between traditional and cyberbullying. All measures of morality were significantly associated with both traditional and cyberbullying, showing a consistent picture and confirming previous research. Both lower commitment to a moral valuing self and lower feelings of remorse predicted higher levels of traditional bullying and cyberbullying, respectively. The predictive effect of moral emotions and moral values on cyberbullying was especially pronounced and remained significant even when traditional bullying was controlled for. In contrast, higher levels of disengaged justifications predicted higher levels of traditional bullying, but were not

TABLE 3
Morality predicting traditional bullying and cyberbullying (tobit regression)

	Traditional bullying	Cyberbullying (1)	Cyberbullying (2)
Age	.004	−.061	−.064
Sex (being male)	.013	−.082	−.088
Disengaged justifications	.161**	.023	−.056
Moral emotions (remorse)	−.273**	−.302**	−.156*
Moral values	−.197**	−.205**	−.115*
Traditional bullying			.454**
Explained variance (R^2)	.248**	.198**	.337**

Notes: Cyberbullying was used twice as dependent variable: without (1) and with (2) controlling for traditional bullying. **$p < .01$; *$p < .05$. Cells show standardized coefficients.

associated with cyberbullying. These findings indicate that in spite of the high overlap between traditional and cyberbullying, and in spite of consistent associations between both bullying forms and morality, differential patterns exist when it comes to associations between moral disengagement, moral emotions and moral values. With respect to moral disengagement, higher levels of disengaged justifications did not predict higher levels of cyberbullying. It seems that not seeing the victim suffer makes the use of cognitive distancing strategies unnecessary instead of making it easier to use these strategies, as Almeida et al. (2008) suggested. Our finding is line with a study by Bauman and Pero (2011), which also reported non-significant associations. However, other studies such as Pornari and Wood (2010) or Bauman (2010) did find significant associations between cyberbullying and moral disengagement. These inconsistencies may be related to different measures and certainly need further exploration in future research.

With respect to moral emotions, the present results suggest pronounced predictive power of remorse on cyberbullying. We may speculate that the absence of direct contact between perpetrator and victim lowers the cyberbully's emotional engagement regarding feelings of remorse. Like empathy, remorse is an indicator of an individual's awareness of the negative consequences of harmful acts for the victim and thus acts as a mediator between moral standards and moral behaviour (cf. Tangney et al., 2007). Moreover, if no remorse is anticipated as a result of harassing others via electronic media (e.g., because the behaviour is in line with a person's lack of moral values), then, of course, disengagement strategies become unnecessary. Thus, our findings for disengagement strategies, moral values and remorse in the context of cyberbullying can be integrated into the same explanatory framework.

Strengths and limitations

In our study we used an online questionnaire. Accordingly, we had no direct control over data quality. As we recruited participants from a population of regular users of a specific student social networking site, we had a self-selected sample of this group of adolescents. Furthermore the study was described as being on "coping with cyberbullying", and victims of bullying were therefore overrepresented in our sample (Perren, 2011).

The sampling procedure used entailed two major drawbacks. First, it meant that parental consent could not be obtained. Although the "terms of use agreement" approach was intended to meet this difficulty, it cannot be regarded as fully corresponding with direct parental consent. However, the most ethical course of action, i.e., gaining parents' written informed consent, is often difficult to accomplish in on-line research (see Stern, 2004). Second, the self-selection of the sample may have resulted in the over- or underrepresentation of critical participant characteristics. Birnbaum (2004) states that data collected in an on-line study cannot be assumed to represent a sample of some stable population of "web users" and that self-selected web participants cannot be assumed to represent random samples of any particular population. In order to jointly address these two issues in future research and still use the internet with its rich potential to better understand adolescents (Stern, 2004), a different approach needs to be developed. One potential solution might be to use a step-by-step procedure including invited accessibility (Nosek, Banaji, & Greenwald, 2002) by contacting a randomly selected sample of participants from a school district and providing them with both a unique access code and a link. In a first step, teachers from a randomly selected sample of classrooms are asked to gain informed consent from parents. Those adolescents for whom parental consent is given constitute a pool from which actual participants are randomly selected and contacted. However, such a procedure means that schools and teachers need to be willing to assist in the research and requires careful embedding of the study within the curriculum, e.g., as an assignment in media competence. By afterwards explaining this sampling procedure and the necessity of obtaining parental consent to all students, teachers can sensitize them to the degree of protection owed to them while they are under age, both generally and with respect to research participation.

One of the strengths of our study is the inclusion of participants from early to late adolescence. However, we did not find expected age trends regarding bullying and morality. Moreover, we did not find moderating effects of age on the investigated associations. This lack of associations might be due to self-selection of participants. Further longitudinal research should tap more into developmental processes. As cyberbullying seems to have a peak in middle adolescence, further studies should also investigate non-linear developmental trends. As this question was beyond the scope of the current study, we only tested linear age trends.

In our study, we used different indicators of morality to explain the occurrence of (cyber)bullying. Although most of the measures include adolescents' self-reports, one strength of our study lies in the use of a production measure to assess adolescents' moral justifications instead of a self-report questionnaire on moral disengagement. For the assessment of morally disengaged justifications and moral emotions we used a scenario approach, i.e., participants indicated their hypothetical cognitions and emotions regarding specific (cyber)aggression situations. This approach was chosen to tap into participants' feelings and cognitions regarding specific situations. As we did aggregate answers from different scenarios, we mainly assessed participants' general proneness to moral disengagement or feelings of remorse. In order to investigate distinct psychological processes that might be associated with cyberbullying versus traditional bullying, future studies should also apply experimental approaches. Such approaches should aim to disentangle the role of specific situational features of cyberbullying (e.g., visibility of the victim) versus the role of personal attitudes (e.g., general proneness to moral disengagement; e.g., Sticca & Perren, 2010).

Conclusion

In sum, our study showed that moral emotions (i.e., reduced feelings of remorse and guilt) and a low commitment to moral values are especially important to explain adolescents' engagement in both traditional and cyberbullying. The results have also implications for prevention and intervention. As both emotional, values-related, and cognitive aspects of morality predicted bullying (and in part cyberbullying), there is a need for integrative approaches to promote moral growth including a deeper understanding of why (cyber)bullying is morally wrong. Accordingly, a "wide range of moral emotions [need to be introduced] into educational practice in a systematic way" (Malti & Latzko, 2010, p. 5) and related both to values-related and cognitive facets of moral functioning. Apart from promoting empathy and perspective taking, moral emotions like guilt and shame, pride, indignation, etc., need to be addressed and contextualized within specific (cyber)bullying situations. Adolescents must be given time and room to question easy and common disengagement-friendly and bullying-friendly classroom norms, attitudes, and interaction styles and to both develop and maintain prosocial norms and values.

REFERENCES

Almeida, A., Marinho, S., Esteves, C., Gomes, S., & Correia, I. (2008). *Virtual but not less real: A study of cyberbullying and its relations with moral disengagement and empathy.* Poster presented at the 20th Biennial ISSBD Meeting, Würzburg, 13–17 July 2008.

Arsenio, W. F., & Lemerise, E. A. (2004). Aggression and moral development: Integrating social information processing and moral domain models. *Child Development, 75*(4), 987–1002.

Bandura, A. (2002). Selective moral disengagement in the exercise of moral agency. *Journal of Moral Education, 31*(2), 101–119.

Bauman, S. (2010). Cyberbullying in a rural intermediate school: An exploratory study. *The Journal of Early Adolescence, 30*(6), 803–833.

Bauman, S., & Pero, H. (2011). Bullying and cyberbullying among deaf students and their hearing peers: An exploratory study. *Journal of Deaf Studies and Deaf Education, 16*(2), 236–253.

Birnbaum, M. H. (2004). Human research and data collection via the internet. *Annual Review of Psychology, 55*, 803–832.

Blasi, A. (2001). Moral motivation and society. Internalization and the development of the self. In G. Dux & F. Welz (Eds.), *Moral und Recht im Diskurs der Moderne* [*Morality and justice in modern age discourse*] (pp. 313–329). Opladen, Germany: Leske + Budrich.

Campbell, K. M. (2004). *Moral identity, youth engagement, and discussions with parents and peers.* St. Catharines, Ontario, Canada: Brock University.

Dooley, J., Pyzalski, J., & Cross, D. (2009). Cyberbullying versus face-to-face bullying. A theoretical and conceptual review. *Zeitschrift für Psychologie/Journal of Psychology, 217*(4), 182–188.

Gini, G. (2006). Social cognition and moral cognition in bullying: What's wrong? *Aggressive Behavior, 32*(6), 528–539.

Gini, G., Pozzoli, T., & Hauser, M. (2011). Bullies have enhanced moral competence to judge relative to victims, but lack moral compassion. *Personality and Individual Differences, 50*(5), 603–608.

Gradinger, P., Strohmeier, D., & Spiel, C. (2009). Traditional bullying and cyberbullying: Identification of risk groups for adjustment problems. *Zeitschrift für Psychologie/Journal of Psychology, 217*(4), 205–213.

Hinduja, S., & Patchin, J. W. (2008). Cyberbullying: An exploratory analysis of factors related to offending and victimization. *Deviant Behavior, 29*(2), 129–156.

Hymel, S., Rocke-Henderson, N., & Bonanno, R. A. (2005). Moral disengagement: A framework for understanding bullying among adolescents. *Journal of Social Sciences, Special Issue No. 8,* 33–43.

Hymel, S., Schonert-Reichl, K. A., Bonanno, R. A., Vaillancourt, T., & Henderson, N. R. (2010). Bullying and morality: Understanding how good kids can behave badly. In S. R. Jimerson, S. M. Swearer, & D. Espelage (Eds.), *The handbook of school bullying: An international perspective* (pp. 101–118). New York, NY: Routledge.

Kline, R. B. (1998). *Principles and practice of structural equation modeling.* New York, NY: Guilford Press.

Krettenauer, T., Malti, T., & Sokol, B. W. (2008). The development of moral emotion expectancies and the happy victimizer phenomenon: A critical review of theory and application. *European Journal of Developmental Science, 2*(3), 221–235.

Laible, D., Eye, J., & Carlo, G. (2008). Dimensions of conscience in mid-adolescence: Links with social behavior, parenting, and temperament. *Journal of Youth and Adolescence, 37*(7), 875–887.

Malti, T., Gasser, L., & Buchmann, M. (2009). Aggressive and prosocial children's emotion attributions and moral reasoning. *Aggressive Behavior, 35*(1), 90–102.

Malti, T., & Latzko, B. (2010). Children's moral emotions and moral cognition: Towards an integrative perspective. *New Directions for Child and Adolescent Development, 2010*(129), 1–10.

Menesini, E., & Camodeca, M. (2008). Shame and guilt as behaviour regulators: Relationships with bullying, victimization and prosocial behaviour. *British Journal of Developmental Psychology, 26*(2), 183–196.

Menesini, E., Sanchez, V., Fonzi, A., Ortega, R., Costabile, A., & Lo Feudo, G. (2003). Moral emotions and bullying: A cross-national comparison of differences between bullies, victims and outsiders. *Aggressive Behavior, 29*(6), 515–530.

Nosek, B. A., Banaji, M. R., & Greenwald, A. G. (2002). E-research: Ethics, security, design, and control in psychological research on the internet. *Journal of Social Issues, 58*(1), 161–176.

Obermann, M. L. (2011). Moral disengagement in self-reported and peer-nominated school bullying. *Aggressive Behavior, 37*(2), 133–144.

Osgood, D. W., Finken, L. L., & McMorris, B. J. (2002). Analyzing multiple-item measures of crime and deviance II: Tobit regression analysis of transformed scores. *Journal of Quantitative Criminology, 18*(4), 319–347.

Paciello, M., Fida, R., Tramontano, C., Lupinetti, C., & Caprara, G. V. (2008). Stability and change of moral disengagement and its impact on aggression and violence in late adolescence. *Child Development, 79*(5), 1288–1309.

Perren, S. (2011). Entwicklungsprobleme im Ablösungs- und Autonomisierungsprozess. In S. Albisser, C. Bieri Buschor, H. Moser, & K. Kansteiner-Schänzlin (Eds.), *Sozialisation- und Entwicklungsaufgaben von Heranwachsenden* (Vol. 1, pp. 179–198). Baltmannsweiler, Germany: Schneider Verlag.

Perren, S., Gutzwiller-Helfenfinger, E., Groeben, M., Stadelmann, S., & von Klitzing, K. (2009). *Bully/victim problems in kindergarten: Are they related to moral disengagement in middle childhood?* Paper presented at the Biennial Meeting of the Society for Research in Child Development, Boston, April 2009.

Perren, S., Gutzwiller-Helfenfinger, E., Malti, T., & Hymel, S. (2011). Moral reasoning and emotion attributions of adolescent bullies, victims, and bully victims. *British Journal of Developmental Psychology.* DOI: 10.1111/j.2044-835X.2011.02059.x.

Perren, S., & Sticca, F. (2011). *Bullying and morality: Are there differences between traditional bullies and cyberbullies?* Poster presented at the SRCD Biennial Meeting, Montréal, March 2011.

Pornari, C. D., & Wood, J. (2010). Peer and cyber aggression in secondary school students: The role of moral disengagement, hostile attribution bias, and outcome expectancies. *Aggressive Behavior, 36*(2), 81–94.

Pratt, M. W., Hunsberger, B., Pancer, M., & Alisat, S. (2003). A longitudinal analysis of personal values socialization: Correlates of a moral self-ideal in late adolescence. *Social Development, 12*(4), 563–585.

Raskauskas, J., & Stoltz, A. D. (2007). Involvement in traditional and electronic bullying among adolescents. *Developmental Psychology, 43*(3), 564–575.

Salmivalli, C., & Voeten, M. (2004). Connections between attitudes, group norms, and behaviour in bullying situations. *International Journal of Behavioral Development, 28*(3), 246–258.

Schwartz, S. H. (2006). Human values: Theory, measurement, and applications. *Revue Française de Sociologie, 47*(4), 249–288.

Slonje, R., & Smith, P. K. (2008). Cyberbullying: Another main type of bullying? *Scandinavian Journal of Psychology, 49*(2), 147–154.

Smith, P. K., Mahdavi, J., Carvalho, M., Fisher, S., Russell, S., & Tippett, N. (2008). Cyberbullying: Its nature and impact in secondary school pupils. *Journal of Child Psychology and Psychiatry, 49*(4), 376–385.

Smith, P. K., & Slonje, R. (2010). Cyberbullying: The nature and extent of a new kind of bullying, in and out of school. In S. R. Jimerson, S. M. Swearer, & D. Espelage (Eds.), *The international handbook of school bullying* (pp. 249–262). Hillsdale, NJ: Lawrence Erlbaum Associates, Inc.

Stassen Berger, K. (2007). Update on bullying at school: Science forgotten? *Developmental Review, 27*(1), 90–126.

Stern, S. (2004). Studying adolescents online: A consideration of ethical issues. In E. A. Buchanan (Ed.), *Readings in virtual research ethics: issues and controversies* (pp. 274–287). Hershey, PA: Idea Group, Inc.

Sticca, F., & Perren, S. (2010). *Guilt and perceived severity in cyber and non-cyber bullying scenarios.* Paper presented at the E-youth Conference, Antwerp.

Tangney, J. P., Stuewig, J., & Mashek, D. J. (2007). Moral emotions and moral behavior. *Psychology, 58*(1), 345–372.

Ttofi, M. M., & Farrington, D. P. (2008). Reintegrative shaming theory, moral emotions and bullying. *Aggressive Behavior, 34*, 352–368.

Cyberbullying in context: Direct and indirect effects by low self-control across 25 European countries

Alexander T. Vazsonyi[1], Hana Machackova[2], Anna Sevcikova[2], David Smahel[2], and Alena Cerna[2]

[1]Department of Family Sciences, University of Kentucky, Lexington, KY, USA
[2]Institute for Research on Children, Youth and Family, Masaryk University, Brno, Czech Republic

Random samples of at least 1,000 youth, ages 9 to 16 years, from 25 European countries ($N = 25,142$) were used to test the salience of low self-control on cyberbullying perpetration and victimization (direct and indirect effects), framed by a cross-cultural developmental approach. Path models, which provided evidence of invariance by sex, tested the hypothesized links among low self-control as well as known correlates, including offline perpetration and victimization, and externalizing behaviours. Results showed positive associations between online and offline bullying behaviours (perpetration and victimization), and, more interestingly, both direct but mostly indirect effects by low self-control on cyberbullying perpetration and victimization; externalizing behaviours had little additional explanatory power. Importantly, multi-group tests by country samples provided evidence of quite modest differences in the tested links across the 25 developmental contexts, despite

Correspondence should be addressed to Alexander T. Vazsonyi, University of Kentucky, Department of Family Sciences, 316 Funkhouser Building, Lexington, KY 40506, USA.
E-mail: vazsonyi@uky.edu

Data collection of the "EU Kids Online" network was funded by the EC (DG Information Society) Safer Internet Plus Programme (project code SIP-KEP-321803); this work was supported by Masaryk University and by a Fulbright-Masaryk Distinguished Chair fellowship to the first author to spend the fall semester (2010) in the Department of Psychology and the Institute for Research on Children, Youth and Family at Masaryk University in Brno (Czech Republic). The remaining authors were supported by the Czech Ministry of Education, Youth and Sports (MSM0021622406), the Czech Science Foundation (P407/11/0585), and the Faculty of Social Studies, Masaryk University. We would like to thank Pan Chen at the University of Chicago for her assistance with conducting the multi-level model test.

some observed differences in the amount of variance explained in the dependent measures.

Keywords: Cyberbullying; Self-control; Deviance; Problem behaviours; Cross-cultural.

INTRODUCTION

Epidemiological data support the widespread existence of cyberbullying perpetration and victimization in the USA (Kowalski & Limber, 2007), Europe (Vandebosch & Van Cleemput, 2009; see also Kiriakidis & Kavoura, 2010; Tokunaga, 2010), and Australia (Spears, Slee, Owens, & Johnson 2009). For instance, the incidence of cyberbullying victimization among 9- to 16-year-olds is 8% (5% on the internet and 3% by mobile calls, texts or video; range: 2% to 14% across European countries); on the other hand, cyberbullying perpetration rates are lower, namely 3% have bullied others on the internet, while 2% have done so by mobile calls, texts or video (Livingstone, Haddon, Görzig, & Ólafsson, 2011). Data from the United States further substantiate the problem; 8% of youth between the ages of 10 and 15 years report having been harassed on the internet monthly or more often (Ybarra, Diener-West, & Lief, 2007). Thus, cyberbullying, defined as an intentional and repetitive aggressive behaviour perpetrated through electronic devices (Smith et al., 2008), has become a public health concern.

However, few studies have tested the aetiology or consequences of these behaviours (David-Ferdon & Feldman Hertz, 2007), particularly across different cultural developmental contexts (cf. Florell, Ang, & Schenck, 2010). Strom and Strom (2005) liken cyberbullying perpetration in particular to other unlawful behaviours, with the explicit goal of threatening or harming others. Therefore, cyberbullying perpetration resembles deviance or deviant conduct—conduct that might be readily explained by precursors of deviance, for instance. Only a handful of studies has linked low self-control to bullying (e.g., Unnever & Cornell, 2003) and victimization (Haynie, Nansel, Eitel, Crump, Saylor, et al., 2001), despite the fact that low self-control has been identified as the single most important predictor of deviance and crime in countless empirical studies since self-control theory was published (Gottfredson & Hirschi, 1990; see also Baumeister & Vohs, 2004, for related conceptual work). Previous work has also shown that cyberbullying is highly associated with traditional bullying (Juvonen & Gross, 2008; Raskauskas & Stoltz, 2007), and is thus, potentially, a parallel manifestation of aggression, of deviance, and of low self-control. Finally, self-control should be construed as a manifestation of self-regulation capacity, known to be linked to externalizing behaviours (e.g., Murray & Kochanska, 2002), a potential concomitant of both traditional and cyberbullying (Hay, Meldrum, & Mann, 2010).

The consequences of being victimized are certainly negative even in the sense that cyberbullying aggravates a victim's maladjusted behaviours (Mitchell, Ybarra, & Finkelhor, 2007). In fact, victims of cyberbullying report significantly higher levels of depressive symptoms than victims of traditional bullying, even when controlling for their involvement in traditional bullying/victimization (Perren, Dooley, Shaw, & Cross, 2010). Furthermore, youth who reported either traditional or cyberbullying were more likely to report suicidal ideation and to attempt suicide (Hinduja & Patchin, 2010).

In the current study, we were interested in developing a greater understanding of how low self-control impacts cyberbullying victimization and perpetration among male and female youth, with a consideration of both externalizing behaviours as well as traditional bullying perpetration and victimization. Some of these links were exploratory in nature, such as the one between low self-control and cyber-victimization, for instance. Despite some observed differences in rates of cyberbullying by sex, theoretically, the same causal model applies to both male and female youth; thus, in addition to testing it across developmental contexts, we were also interested in examining its tenability by sex.

The salience of low self-control

Self-control theory (Gottfredson & Hirschi, 1990) identifies key developmental precursors that differentiate between individuals, both males and females, who develop adequate levels of self-control and thus are more likely to conform to social norms, mores, and prescribed behaviours versus ones who do not. Parents and caregivers instil conformity during the first decade of life, instil self-control by maintaining an affectively close bond to their children, by monitoring their behaviours, and by correcting norm violations. These efforts are then also followed up by ones at school in that teachers further build these bonds to society or potentially attempt to correct inadequate early efforts to establish them. The empirical evidence has largely supported this (e.g., Vazsonyi & Huang, 2010).

Individuals low in self-control seek immediate pleasure without much consideration of long-term consequences of their behaviours or actions. Duckworth and Kern (2011) recently conducted a meta-analysis of work testing the operationalization and measurement of self-control and found strong support for the construct. However, they also lament that "several authors have noted the challenge of defining and measuring self-control (also referred to as self-regulation, self-discipline, willpower, effortful control, ego strength, and inhibitory control, among other terms) and its converse, impulsivity or impulsiveness" (p. 259). They also find that researchers across disciplines, such as developmental or personality psychology, generally do not cite or inform each other's efforts. They conclude with a common operational definition that encapsulates developmental efforts on self-regulation of young children as well as work on assessing impulsivity, namely that "self-control is the idea of voluntary self-governance in the service of personally valued goals and standards" (p. 260). In this sense, low self-control is part and parcel of missing self-regulation capacity among children, of poor executive functioning, of poor attentional processes, of sensation seeking or of impulsivity.

We hypothesized that for both male and female adolescents, individuals relatively lower in self-control would be more likely to engage in cyberbullying perpetration as compared to their peers. Taking into account self-control as a predictor of victimization (Haynie et al., 2001) and the significant and substantial overlap of conventional bullying and cyberbullying (offline victimization predicts online victimization; Raskauskas & Stoltz, 2007), we also hypothesized both direct as well as indirect effects on cyberbullying victimization by self-control (via externalizing behaviours, offline perpetration and victimization), again for both male and female youth. Additionally, testing the links between low self-control and cyber-perpetration/victimization might be particularly relevant when considering features of the internet. It is known that online anonymity supports disinhibited conduct (Suler, 2004); in fact, this provides an important opportunity (Gottfredson & Hirschi, 1990) to engage in aggression directed towards others, something simply less likely in the "real world".

Correlates and predictors of cyberbullying perpetration and victimization

Prior research has shown that traditional school bullying predicts cyberbullying. Juvonen and Gross (2008) found that school bullying experiences increased the likelihood of cyberbullying, independently of the type of electronic media used. However, this link is not straightforward. Some research has found that due to online anonymity, youth who are targets of peer aggression at school might in fact seek to retaliate on the internet (Heirman & Walrave, 2008). Research substantiates this and has shown that cyber perpetrators are in fact frequently identified as victims of traditional bullying (Kowalski, Limber, & Agatston, 2008; Li, 2007), or that traditional bully victims tend to bully others online (Smith et al., 2008).

On the other hand, and more salient perhaps, is the evidence which shows that traditional bullying or perpetration predicts the same roles in cyberbullying. Offline peer victimization is also related to cyber-victimization (Hinduja & Patchin, 2008; Raskauskas & Stoltz, 2007; Smith et al., 2008). Furthermore, studies have shown how victimization and perpetration are inextricably linked; a large proportion of those who are cyber-victims are also cyber-aggressors (Hinduja & Patchin, 2007; Sevcikova & Smahel, 2009; Vandebosch & Van Cleemput, 2009; Ybarra & Mitchell, 2004; Ybarra, Mitchell, Wolak, & Finkelhor, 2006). Thus, in our hypothesized model, we tested the relationships not only between traditional perpetration and cyber-perpetration and between traditional victimization and cyber-victimization, but also the paths from traditional bullying to cyber-victimization and from traditional victimization to cyber-perpetration. Quasi antecedent to these relationships, we hypothesized that low self-control would predict both traditional bullying perpetration and victimization, and through them, the two cyberbullying measures.

A number of studies have documented the relationships between aggression and cyberbullying (Ang, Tan, & Mansor, 2011; Aricak, Siyahhan, Uzunhasanoglu, Saribeyoglu, Ciplak, et al., 2008; Calvete, Orue, Estévez, Villardón, & Padilla, 2010; Dilmaç, 2009) or other measures of problem behaviours, as well as between delinquency and cyberbullying (Hinduja & Patchin, 2007, 2008). Thus, we were interested in understanding to what extent self-control explained variability in cyberbullying victimization and perpetration, net any effects by known correlates, including externalizing behaviours (i.e., drinking or delin-quency; Liu, 2004; Stoff, Breiling, & Maser, 1997). We expected that youth growing up during the digital age might spend unsupervised time online placing them at greater risk for cyberbullying, both victimization (Smith et al., 2008) and perpetration (Aricak et al., 2008; Li, 2007). In addition, previous research has shown that externalizing behaviours predict peer victimization (e.g., Hodges, Boivin, Vitaro, & Bukowski, 1999). Thus, the hypothesized model included paths from externalizing behaviours to both cyberbullying perpetration and victimization, but also direct ones from low self-control.

Plan of analysis

Model tests were conducted as path analyses with observed variables in AMOS 18 (Arbuckle, 2009), which permitted us to specify these hypothesized links. In addition, this analytic approach permitted us to test to what extent the observed relationships varied by sex and also whether they replicated across the 25 different European developmental contexts. Customary model fit evaluative criteria provided by AMOS as well as difference statistics were used for this purpose (χ^2, *CFI, NFI, RMSEA*). Observed differences in rates of cyberbullying by country might lead to the erroneous conclusion that the underlying aetiology is unique among males and females or in each developmental context. It is conceivable that despite observed differences in the frequency of these behaviours by sex or across contexts, the underlying aetiology or patterns of associations among known correlates and predictors is largely the same. By applying a rigorous multi-group test, we were able to directly address these questions.[1]

METHODS

Sample and procedures

The present study used data from part of the EU Kids Online II study, which randomly sampled 1,000 youth in each of 25 European countries. This study was conducted in April/October 2010 across these countries and included 25,142 youth (50% girls). It focused on youth between the ages of 9 and 16 years of age. Data were collected through surveys at the homes of participants, after initial pilot tests to ensure understanding. Ipsos MORI provided support for the questionnaire design and contracted with local fieldwork agencies to ensure that a standard approach was used across countries. In each household, a youth and one of his/her parents were asked about the child's online experiences. An informed consent process from both parents and youth was used, and participants were both assured of confidentiality. The study was approved by the LSE (London School of Economics and Political Science) Ethics Committee. Additional details about the study methodology, including human subjects issues, can be consulted online (Linvingstone et al., 2011).

TABLE 1
Descriptive statistics of main study variables by sex

	No. of items	M	SD	Min./ Max.	α	N
Cyberbullying victimization	3	0.10/0.13	0.47/0.53	0/4	–	12,641/12,501
Offline victimization	2	0.24/0.22	0.72/0.70	0/4	–	12,641/12,501
Cyberbullying perpetration	3	0.06/0.06	0.35/0.34	0/4	–	12,641/12,501
Offline perpetration	2	0.17/0.13	0.59/0.50	0/4	–	12,641/12,501
Low self-control	3	1.45/1.33	0.48/0.41	1/3	.62/.58	12,061/12,480
Externalizing behaviours	5	0.11/0.08	0.20/0.18	0/1	.63/.62	12,050/11,984

Note: Values are for male/female youth.

---

[1] We should note that we tested potential age effects on the two dependent measures by adding age as a predictor of them; although it was statistically significant, the size of the effects were very modest (βs $= 0.05$ and 0.03, respectively), and, more importantly, the addition of age did not materially affect the remainder of the model tested (fit or parameter estimates). Thus, for parsimony, we omitted age in model tests.

Measures

We present descriptive statistics of the main scales and variables in Table 1 by sex, including reliability estimates.

Age. Parents were asked the question "What is the age of your child?" and answered about their age in years; parents also had the option of answering "I don't know".

Sex. The child's sex was coded by the interviewer.

Offline and cyberbullying victimization. These were introduced to participants by first describing these behaviours very concretely at the beginning of relevant survey sections ("Sometimes children or teenagers say or do hurtful or nasty things to someone and this can often be quite a few times on different days over a period of time, for example"). Additional examples were provided to cue youth into the behaviours being assessed. Next, a filter question was provided, namely, "Has someone acted in this kind of hurtful or nasty way to you in the PAST 12 MONTHS?" Next, a question assessed the location of the experience, coded as "In person face to face" (offline victimization) or "on the internet" or "by mobile phone calls, texts or image/video texts" (both coded as online or cyberbullying victimization). Finally, a frequency question ascertained how often this happened, on a 4-point Likert-type scale ranging from 1 "*Less often* (than once or twice a month)" to 4 "*Every day or almost every day*". A higher score indicated more frequent victimization experiences.

The final offline and cyberbullying victimization scores were computed by forming a product term between the frequency question and the "location" questions just described, which resulted in a 5-point distribution of scores of offline victimization and cyberbullying victimization, with a preponderance of zeros. To address this high positive skew (3.6 and 5.3, respectively) and to normalize the data, we attempted a series of transformation (log, square root, and reflected inverse); an arbitrary whole number was added to each score (+ 1) to permit the application of these transformations. The inverse improved scores the most (2.4 and 3.8, respectively), but skew remained an issue. However, previous comparative work based on large samples has shown that regression-based techniques as applied in Structural Equation Modeling (SEM) largely provide robust parameter estimates, despite violations of normality (Vazsonyi, Pickering, Junger, & Hessing, 2001). This was largely confirmed and a decision was made to retain the original scores for path analyses. The same process was followed for both perpetration scores as well as externalizing behaviours.

Offline and cyberbullying perpetration. These were identified by the following question: "Have you acted in a way that might have felt hurtful or nasty to someone else in the PAST 12 MONTHS?" Next, a location question identified where the experience took place (as described for the victimization variables), followed by a frequency rating ranging from 1 "*Less often* (than once or twice a month)" to 4 "*Every day or almost every day*". Higher scores indicated more frequent perpetration experiences.

Low self-control. Low self-control was measured by three items for the purpose of the current study, namely, "I get very angry and often lose my temper", "I do dangerous things for fun", "I do exciting things, even if they are dangerous". Statements were answered on the scale 1 "*Not true*", 2 "*A bit true*", and 3 "*Very true*". A scale score was computed by averaging the three items, where a high score indicated low self-control.

Externalizing behaviours. These behaviours were assessed by asking participants about engaging in a variety of problem or antisocial behaviours during the past 12 months; the scale was adapted from the Health Behaviour in School-aged Children survey (HBSC; Currie, Molcho, Boyce, Holstein, Torsheim, et al., 2008) and newly developed for the current study. The five items used included questions about drinking, problems with school attendance, having sexual intercourse, problematic behaviour at school, and trouble with police. Respondents rated the items as 0 "*No*" and 1 "*Yes*". Items were averaged and a high score indicated higher levels of externalizing behaviours.

RESULTS

Cyberbullying rates across Europe

The rates of cyberbullying perpetration and victimization were not the goal of this article, and we do not report them because of space constraints. However, rates across European countries (based on the same data) are described in the report of EU Kids Online II project and are available online.

Correlations of main constructs

Table 2 includes the associations between the main study constructs by sex. In general, the observed associations were consistent with expectations; low self-control was positively associated with externalizing behaviour, but also with both offline and cyberbullying perpetration and victimization. Furthermore, externalizing behaviours were positively associated with each of the perpetration and victimization measures. Finally, the largest associations were found between offline perpetration and cyberbullying perpetration and between offline victimization and cyberbullying victimiza-

TABLE 2
Correlations between main study variables by sex

	1	2	3	4	5	6
1. Cyberbullying victimization		.35	.27	.17	.11	.14
2. Offline victimization	.41		.14	.30	.14	.11
3. Cyberbullying perpetration	.27	.15		.35	.16	.18
4. Offline perpetration	.18	.30	.37		.24	.22
5. Low self-control	.16	.15	.17	.22		.36
6. Externalizing behaviours	.13	.08	.16	.16	.33	

Note: All correlations are significant at .01 level (2-tailed). Values are above the diagonal for male youth and below it for female youth.

tion. Importantly, few differences in the general patterns of associations were found when comparing male and female youth, although some differences in the magnitude of the links were observed. Because of these differences, we were interested in testing the specified path model by sex using a multi-group analysis in AMOS.

Path analysis

In Table 3, we provide the results from multi-group tests by sex (see Figure 1), to examine the extent to which the specified model and links were similar or different for male versus female youth. To do so, we compared an unconstrained to a constrained model, but also conducted path-by-path comparisons to be conservative. Overwhelmingly, the data provided evidence of few differences in the links between constructs for males versus females. This was true of both the chi-square difference tests (not significant in 6 of 11 paths), but certainly also of alternative fit indices (Bentler, 1990; Bentler & Bonett, 1980; Browne & Cudeck, 1993; Cheung & Rensvold, 2002; Meade, Johnson, & Braddy, 2006), which provided evidence of few or no differences between unconstrained and constrained models. It is important to note that chi-square difference tests are considered weak or even inappropriate tests as they are overly sensitive to sample size (Meade et al., 2006); this was certainly the case here with over 10,000 youth in each group. Based on these findings, the remaining analyses were conducted on the total sample.

Table 4 includes the findings from testing the model on the total sample. We only highlight the most salient findings. First, all hypothesized links were significant and in the expected direction. Second, the model explained 15.5% of the total variance in cyberbullying victimization and 13.4% in cyberbullying perpetration. Next, the direct effects by low self-control on cyberbullying victimization and perpetration were significant, yet modest

TABLE 3
Model tests by sex

Model tests	χ^2	df	p	CFI	NFI	RMSEA	$\Delta\chi^2$	Δdf	$p\Delta\chi^2$	ΔCFI	ΔNFI	$\Delta RMSEA$
Unconstrained model	392.997	4	.000	.977	.976	.062						
All paths constrained	576.295	15	.000	.966	.965	.039	183.298	11	.000	.011	.011	.023
b1	398.291	5	.000	.976	.976	.056	5.294	1	.021	.001	.000	.006
b2	397.292	5	.000	.976	.976	.056	4.295	1	.038	.001	.000	.006
b3	423.071	5	.000	.975	.975	.058	30.074	1	.000	.002	.001	.004
b4	393.064	5	.000	.977	.976	.056	0.067	1	.796	.000	.000	.006
b5	470.820	5	.000	.972	.972	.061	77.823	1	.000	.005	.004	.006
b6	417.134	5	.000	.975	.975	.057	24.137	1	.000	.002	.001	.001
b7	396.403	5	.000	.976	.976	.056	3.406	1	.065	.001	.000	.005
b8	395.695	5	.000	.977	.976	.056	2.698	1	.100	.000	.000	.006
b9	393.400	5	.000	.977	.976	.056	0.403	1	.526	.000	.000	.006
b10	393.007	5	.000	.977	.976	.056	0.010	1	.921	.000	.000	.006
b11	393.011	5	.000	.977	.976	.056	0.014	1	.907	.000	.000	.006

Note: Three decimals are shown as differences between nested models are meaningful at third decimal. Δ = values report difference between unconstrained and constrained models.

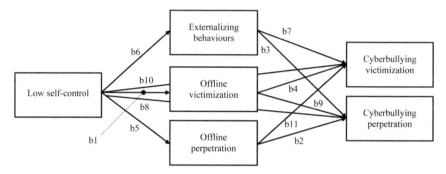

Figure 1. Path model. *Notes*: Error terms of the offline bullying constructs and the error terms of the two cyberbullying measures were allowed to correlate and are not shown in the figure. Path labels (b1–b11) used for the multi-group analysis findings are presented in Table 5; path labels for the multi-group test presented in Table 3 are different from Figure 1 and are available from the first author on request.

TABLE 4
Path coefficients for total sample

Model path			b	SE	β	CR	p
Low self-control	→	Offline victimization	0.232	0.010	0.147	23.590	.000
Low self-control	→	Offline perpetration	0.287	0.008	0.235	38.257	.000
Low self-control	→	Externalizing behaviours	0.150	0.003	0.349	57.834	.000
Offline perpetration	→	Cyberbullying perpetration	0.197	0.004	0.315	50.032	.000
Externalizing behaviours	→	Cyberbullying perpetration	0.148	0.011	0.083	12.888	.000
Offline victimization	→	Cyberbullying victimization	0.252	0.004	0.358	58.691	.000
Externalizing behaviours	→	Cyberbullying victimization	0.190	0.016	0.074	11.629	.000
Offline perpetration	→	Cyberbullying victimization	0.032	0.006	0.036	5.743	.000
Low self-control	→	Cyberbullying victimization	0.049	0.007	0.044	6.877	.000
Low self-control	→	Cyberbullying perpetration	0.041	0.005	0.054	8.357	.000
Offline victimization	→	Cyberbullying perpetration	0.018	0.003	0.038	6.104	.000

(βs = 0.04 and 0.05). However, more substantial overall indirect effects by low self-control on cyberbullying victimization and perpetration (i.e., via externalizing behaviours, offline perpetration/victimization) were found (βs = 0.09 and 0.11). Fourth, model fit, generally not an important consideration in path models with only observed variables, was quite good: $\chi^2(2) = 395.098$; *CFI* and *NFI* = .976; *RMSEA* = .088. Finally, consistent with expectations, offline and cyberbullying behaviours (victimization to victimization, perpetration to perpetration) were strongly associated (βs = 0.36 and 0.32, respectively), although only sharing 10 to 13% of the variance.

Multi-group model test. In a final step, we were interested in under-standing to what extent the hypothesized relationships varied by study country. For this purpose, a series of multi-group model tests were conducted. Again, an unconstrained model was compared to a fully constrained model, with follow-up path-by-path tests (paths b1 to b11; Figure 1). Findings from these model tests are shown in Table 5. The fully constrained model significantly differed from the unconstrained model, based both on the significance test as well as alternative fit indices (*CFI, NFI, RMSEA*). However, follow-up tests path by path (b1 to b11), although again significantly different based on the chi-square difference test, provided evidence of modest differences across country samples, based on inspection of changes in alternative fit indices. These differences were very small in magnitude (*ΔCFI, ΔNFI, ΔRMSEA*), thus permitting a general conclusion that when considering each of the 11 individuals paths tested, results provide support for similarities in the hypothesized paths across the 25 samples (Cheung & Rensvold, 2002; Meade et al., 2006). It is important to note that some paths did seem less similar (or more different) than others across the samples, particularly paths b2 and b4, namely the links between offline and cyberbullying behaviours. Also, when evaluating indirect effects by low self-control on the two dependent measures, differences were found in magnitude across countries, range: .017 (Denmark) to .168 (France) and .044 (Netherlands) to .149 (Cyprus) for perpetration and victimization, respectively. Similarly, the amount of variance explained varied across developmental contexts (14.3% and 16.5% for perpetration and victimiza-tion, respectively; additional details are available upon request).[2]

DISCUSSION

Cyberbullying has become a widespread problem with the arrival of new media and readily available access to the internet. National figures across the 25 European study countries suggest that a substantial proportion of school-age youth are both engaged in perpetrating bullying online or over the phone, and even a larger number of school-age children report having

---

[2] In a final exploratory analytic step, we wanted to understand to what extent our findings might be a function of sample nesting effects; in other words, do we find level 2 variability in the dependent measures, and to what extent do model predictors explain some of this variance. Thus, we examined both an unconditional and a conditional multi-level model in SPSS. Two findings require mention. First, there was very little between-country variability (ICC), namely 0.5% for cyberbullying perpetration and 1% for cyberbullying victimization. Second, we found both fixed and random effects by low self-control on the two dependent measures, and, very importantly, the between-country variance became non-significant once low self-control was added into a conditional model, thus indicating that the very modest level 2 variance in cyberbullying measures was fully explained by low self-control.

TABLE 5
Multi-group model tests: Comparisons across 25 European countries

Model tests	χ^2	df	p	CFI	NFI	RMSEA	$\Delta\chi^2$	Δdf	$p\Delta\chi^2$	ΔCFI	ΔNFI	$\Delta RMSEA$
Unconstrained model	643.304	50	.000	.968	.966	.022						
Fully constrained model	2845.641	314	.000	.864	.851	.018	2202.337	264	.000	.104	.115	.004
b1	714.300	74	.000	.966	.963	.019	70.996	24	.000	.002	.003	.003
b2	1163.818	74	.000	.941	.939	.024	520.515	24	.000	.027	.027	-.002
b3	790.727	74	.000	.961	.959	.020	147.423	24	.000	.007	.007	.002
b4	1181.166	74	.000	.940	.938	.024	537.863	24	.000	.028	.028	-.002
b5	808.455	74	.000	.960	.958	.020	165.151	24	.000	.008	.008	.002
b6	824.465	74	.000	.960	.957	.020	181.162	24	.000	.008	.009	.002
b7	740.233	74	.000	.964	.961	.019	96.929	24	.000	.004	.005	.003
b8	693.426	74	.000	.967	.964	.018	50.122	24	.001	.001	.002	.004
b9	807.552	74	.000	.961	.958	.020	164.248	24	.000	.007	.008	.002
b10	680.252	74	.000	.967	.964	.018	36.948	24	.044	.001	.004	.004
b11	737.410	74	.000	.964	.961	.019	94.106	24	.000	.004	.005	.003

Notes: Model fit for unconstrained model, fully constrained model (all paths constrained to equality across countries) and models with individual paths constrained to equality across all countries. Three decimals shown in this table as differences between nested models meaningful at third decimal. Δ = values reporting difference between unconstrained and constrained models.

been affected by these behaviours. Despite a growing body of studies in this area, as is often the case, our knowledge base and how to address this issue seems to lag behind. To gain a better understanding of how to address these behaviours, the initial step must include knowledge building related to the aetiology of cyberbullying behaviours.

This is precisely how this study sought to advance our understanding of these behaviours. Our unique focus on the importance of low self-control is related to the insight that bullying behaviours, regardless of modus or locale, are forms of norm violations or deviant acts committed against other individuals. In this sense, these behaviours are potential parallels to violence perpetration and victimization, for instance. One of most consistent constructs identified theoretically and confirmed empirically over the past two decades is low self-control, based both on self-control theory (Gottfredson & Hirschi, 1990) and on psychological work (Baumeister & Vohs, 2004; Duckworth, 2011). Recent work continues to bring attention to the importance of low self-control not only for norm violations, but also for a variety of adjustment indicators over the life course (e.g., Moffitt, Arseneault, Belsky, Dickson, Hancox, et al., 2011). This also includes seminal work by Duckworth and Kern (2011), which solidifies self-control as a construct, despite different nomenclature used across a number of social scientific disciplines. Our study adds to this existing literature on the importance of self-control by establishing its links with cyberbullying perpetration and victimization.

The evidence points out the salience of indirect effects by low self-control on cyberbullying. For cyberbullying perpetration, low self-control has a moderate effect on offline bullying perpetration, which is linked to cyberbullying perpetration. Not surprisingly, we found that the effect by low self-control is smaller for victimization measures.

Extant data indicate inconsistencies in rates of cyberbullying among male and female youth across Europe, although victimization rates are higher among females (Kowalski & Limber, 2007); this is so despite the fact that female adolescents are known to have higher levels of self-control (DeLisi, Beaver, Vaughn, Trulson, Kosloski, et al., 2010). This might provide some support for the hypothesis that opportunity plays an important role in our understanding these behaviours (Gottfredson & Hirschi, 1990). With the current level of penetration by mobile phones and the internet, opportunities for cyberbullying are ever present for both males and females; thus, we might expect to find few differences in the use of these media. Furthermore, this is consistent with our findings that the effect by self-control on cyberbullying perpetration is mostly indirect, and it is possible that the disinhibition effect (Heirman & Walrave, 2008; Suler, 2004) simply plays a more important role among female perpetrators. Future work will be needed to further address this question.

Also, although we find higher victimization rates among female youth, the cyberbullying perpetration rates among male and female youth across Europe are not consistent (Livingstone et al., 2011). Importantly, we did not find significant differences between male and female youth in the links between low self-control and both cyberbullying perpetration and victimization. Again, this might point to the salience of opportunity.

Cyberbullying does not seem to be a behaviour problem that is independent from traditional bullying in that offline victims are also at risk to be the victims online; in addition, offline perpetrators seem to be at greater risk to be perpetrators online (Hinduja & Patchin, 2008; Juvonen & Gross, 2008; Raskauskas & Stoltz, 2007; Smith et al., 2008). As low self-control clearly impacts cyberbullying, and because this effect was mostly indirect through correlates, we might conclude that cyberbullying simply seems to be a specific form of traditional bullying, and thus require little unique explanatory effort. But, with regard to our other findings, cyberbullying does seem to have some specific features that make it a unique kind of behaviour and experience worthy of inquiry.

Although our model was generally supported by the data, and invariant across the 25 country samples, it is important to note that the amount of variance explained in the two cyberbullying constructs was quite modest (about 10 to 20% across country samples). Also, our findings do not preclude the possibility that there exist country-specific differences regarding socialization processes—and thus, the development of self-control—which, in combination with a consideration of opportunity, might partly explain some observed differences. Future research needs to further examine the role played by parenting or other socialization mechanisms as well as the importance of potential sex differences in media use.

Study findings need to be considered with its limitations in mind. First, our measurement of cyberbullying was effectively based on a single-item approach, thus calling into question the validity of these measures. Second, a large number of participants apparently simply did not reply to some of the more sensitive questions related to being victimized or perpetrating bullying, thus necessitating the assumption analytically that they were neither perpetrators nor victims of cyberbullying. Future work should employ greater breadth in assessment as well as mechanisms by which participants are required to provide information about whether they have engaged in cyberbullying perpetration or have been victimized. Related to this, future work should also engage in a greater in-depth analysis of potential age effects on the observed relationships. Next, the current study was simply based on cross-sectional data, and thus no causal inferences can be made, despite an inherent directionality part of the specified path model tested. Specifically, a model could also be supported by the data where externalizing behaviours predict cyberbullying, for instance. Finally, given the relatively modest variance we explained, future studies should reconsider more broadly the factors that provide promise to explain cyberbullying and to provide a greater understanding to preconditions for the development and implementation of effective prevention and intervention efforts.

In conclusion, we find the evidence compelling on the invariant patterns across the 25 European cultures, but also for male versus female youth. Furthermore, the manner in which low self-control indirectly explains variance in cyberbullying victimization and cyberbullying perpetration shows some measure of promise for areas to address and potentially remedy these quasi epidemic behaviour problems facing youth today. At the same time, we find equally impressive the unexplained amount of variance, suggesting that much remains to be learned in this area of inquiry.

REFERENCES

Ang, R. P., Tan, K. A., & Mansor, A. T. (2011). Normative beliefs about aggression as a mediator of narcissistic exploitativeness and cyberbullying. *Journal of Interpersonal Violence, 26*(13), 2619–2634.

Arbuckle, J. L. (2009). *Amos 18 user's guide*. Chicago, IL: Amos Development Corporation.

Aricak, T., Siyahhan, S., Uzunhasanoglu, A., Saribeyoglu, S., Ciplak, S., Yilmaz, Y., et al. (2008). Cyberbullying among Turkish adolescents. *Cyberpsychology and Behavior, 11*(3), 253–261.

Baumeister, R. F., & Vohs, K. D. (2004). *Handbook of self-regulation: Research, theory, and applications*. New York, NY: Guilford Press.

Bentler, P M. (1990). Comparative fit indexes in structural models. *Psychological Bulletin, 107*, 238–246.

Bentler, P. M., & Bonett, D. G. (1980). Significant tests and goodness of fit in the analysis of covariance structures. *Psychological Bulletin, 88*, 588–606.

Browne, M. W., & Cudeck, R. (1993). Alternative ways of assessing model fit. In K. A. Bollen & J. S. Long (Eds.), *Testing structural equation models* (pp. 136–162). Newbury Park, CA: Sage.

Calvete, E., Orue, I., Estévez, A., Villardón, L., & Padilla, P. (2010). Cyberbullying in adolescents: Modalities and aggressors' profile. *Computers in Human Behavior, 26*, 1128–1135.

Cheung, G. W., & Rensvold, R. B. (2002). Evaluating goodness-of-fit indexes for testing measurement invariance. *Structural Equation Modeling, 9*, 233–255.

Currie, C., Molcho, M., Boyce, W., Holstein, B., Torsheim, T., Richter, M. (2008). Researching health inequalities in adolescents: The development of the Health Behaviour in School-Aged Children (HBSC) Family Affluence Scale. *Social Science & Medicine, 66*, 1429–1436.

David-Ferdon, C., & Feldman Hertz, M. (2007). Electronic media, violence, and adolescents: An emerging public health problem. *Journal of Adolescent Health, 41*, S1–S5.

DeLisi, M., Beaver, K. M., Vaughn, M. G., Trulson, C. R., Kosloski, A. E., Drury, A. J., et al. (2010). Personality, gender, and self-control theory revisited: Results from a sample of institutionalized juvenile delinquents. *Applied Psychology in Criminal Justice, 6*(1), 31–46.

Dilmaç, B. (2009). Psychological needs as a predictor of cyberbullying: A preliminary report on college students. *Educational Sciences: Theory & Practice, 9*(3), 1291–1325.

Duckworth, A. L. (2011). The significance of self-control. *Proceedings of the National Academy of Sciences, 108*(7), 2639–2640.

Duckworth, A. L., & Kern, M. L. (2011). A meta-analysis of the convergent validity of self-control measures. *Journal of Research in Personality, 45*(3), 259–268.

Florell, D., Ang, R., & Schenck, C. (2010, February). *Proactive and reactive aggression in cyberbullying: An international comparison.* Poster presented at the National Association of School Psychologists (NASP) Annual National Conference, Chicago, IL.

Gottfredson, M. R., & Hirschi, T. (1990). *General theory of crime.* Stanford, CA: Stanford University Press.

Hay, C., Meldrum, R., & Mann, K. (2010). Traditional bullying, cyber bullying, and deviance: A general strain theory approach. *Journal of Contemporary Criminal Justice, 26*(2), 130–147.

Haynie, D. L., Nansel, T., Eitel, P., Crump, A. D., Saylor, K., Yu, K., et al. (2001). Bullies, victims, and bully/victims: Distinct groups of at-risk youth. *Journal of Early Adolescence, 21*(1), 29–49.

Heirman, W., & Walrave, M. (2008). Assessing concerns and issues about the mediation of technology in cyberbullying. *Cyberpsychology: Journal of Psychosocial Research on Cyberspace, 2*(2). (Retrieved from http://www.cyberpsychology.eu/view.php?cisloclanku=20 08111401)

Hinduja, S., & Patchin, J. W. (2007). Offline consequences of online victimization: School violence and delinquency. *Journal of School Violence, 6*(3), 89–212.

Hinduja, S., & Patchin, J. W. (2008). Cyberbullying: An exploratory analysis of factors related to offending and victimization. *Deviant Behavior, 29*, 129–156.

Hinduja, S., & Patchin, J. W. (2010). Bullying, cyberbullying, and suicide. *Archives of Suicide Research, 14*(3), 206–221.

Hodges, E., Boivin, M., Vitaro, F., & Bukowski, W. M. (1999). The power of friendship: Protection against an escalating cycle of peer victimization. *Developmental Psychology, 35*, 94–101.

Juvonen, J., & Gross, E. F. (2008). Extending the school grounds? Bullying experiences in cyberspace. *Journal of School Health, 78*, 496–505.

Kiriakidis, S. P., & Kavoura, A. (2010). A review of the literature on harassment through the internet and other electronic means. *Family and Community Health, 33*(2), 82–93.

Kowalski, R. N., & Limber, S. P. (2007). Electronic bullying among middle school students. *Journal of Adolescent Health, 41*, S22–S30.

Kowalski, R. N., Limber, S. P., & Agatston, W. P. (2008). *Cyberbullying: Bullying in the digital age.* Malden, MA: Blackwell Publishing.

Li, Q. (2007). New bottle but old wine: A research of cyberbullying in schools. *Computers in Human Behavior, 23*, 1777–1791.

Liu, J. (2004). Childhood externalizing behavior: Theory and implications. *Journal of Child and Adolescent Psychiatric Nursing, 17*(3), 93–103.

Livingstone, S., Haddon, L., Görzig, A., & Ólafsson, K., with members of the EU Kids Online network. (2011). *Risks and safety on the internet. The perspective of European children. Full findings and policy implications from the EU Kids Online survey of 9–16 year olds and their parents in 25 countries.* (Retrieved from: http://www2.lse.ac.uk/media@lse/research/EUKids Online/EUKidsII%20(2009–11)/EUKidsOnlineIIReports/D4FullFindings.pdf)

Meade, A. W., Johnson, E. C., & Braddy, P. W. (2006, August). *The utility of alternative fit indices in tests of measurement invariance.* Paper presented at the Annual Academy of Management Conference, Atlanta, GA.

Mitchell, K. J., Ybarra, M., & Finkelhor, D. (2007). The relative importance of online victimization in understanding depression, delinquency, and substance use. *Child Maltreatment, 12*, 314–324.

Moffitt, T. E., Arseneault, L., Belsky, D., Dickson, N., Hancox, R. J., Harrington, H., et al. (2011). A gradient of childhood self-control predicts health, wealth, and public safety. *Proceedings of the National Academy of Sciences, 108*(7), 2693–2698.

Murray, K. T., & Kochanska, G. (2002). Effortful control: Factor structure and relation to externalizing and internalizing behaviors. *Journal of Abnormal Child Psychology, 30,* 503–514.

Perren, S., Dooley, J., Shaw, T., & Cross, D. (2010). Bullying in school and cyberspace: Associations with depressive symptoms in Swiss and Australian adolescents. *Child and Adolescent Psychiatry and Mental Health, 4*(28), 1–10.

Raskauskas, J., & Stoltz, A. D. (2007). Involvement in traditional and electronic bullying among adolescents. *Developmental Psychology, 43,* 564–575.

Sevcikova, A., & Smahel, D. (2009). Online harassment and cyberbullying in the Czech Republic: Comparison across age. *Zeitschrift für Psychologie, 217,* 227–229.

Smith, P. K., Mahdavi, J., Carvalho, M., Fisher, S., Russell, S., & Tippett, N. (2008). Cyberbullying: Its nature and impact in secondary school pupils. *Journal of Child Psychology and Psychiatry, 49*(4), 376–385.

Spears, B., Slee, P., Owens, L., & Johnson, B. (2009). Behind the scenes and screens: Insights into the human dimension of covert and cyberbullying. *Zeitschrift für Psychologie/Journal of Psychology, 217,* 189–196.

Stoff, D., Breiling, J., & Maser, J. (1997). *Handbook of antisocial behavior.* New York, NY: Wiley.

Strom, P. S., & Strom, R. D. (2005). Cyberbullying by adolescents: A preliminary assessment. *The Educational Forum, 70,* 21–32.

Suler, J. (2004). The online disinhibition effect. *Cyberpsychology and Behavior, 7*(3), 321–326.

Tokunaga, R. S. (2010). Following you home from school: A critical review and synthesis of research on cyberbullying victimization. *Computers in Human Behavior, 26,* 277–287.

Unnever, J., & Cornell, D. G. (2003). Bullying, self control, and ADHD. *Journal of Interpersonal Violence, 18,* 129–147.

Vandebosch, H., & Van Cleemput, K. (2009). Cyberbullying among youngsters: Profiles of bullies and victims. *New Media Society, 11*(8), 1349–1371.

Vazsonyi, A. T., & Huang, L. (2010). Where self-control comes from: On the development of self-control and its relationship to deviance over time. *Developmental Psychology, 46*(1), 245–257.

Vazsonyi, A. T., Pickering, L. E., Junger, M., & Hessing, D. (2001). An empirical test of a general theory of crime: A four-nation comparative study of self-control and the prediction of deviance. *Journal of Research in Crime and Delinquency, 38*(2), 91–131.

Ybarra, M. L., Diener-West, M., & Lief, P. J. (2007). Examining the overlap in internet harassment and school bullying: Implications for school intervention. *Journal of Adolescent Health, 41,* S42–S50.

Ybarra, M. L., & Mitchell, K. J. (2004). Online aggressor/targets, aggressors, and targets: A comparison of associated youth characteristics. *Journal of Child Psychology & Psychiatry, 45,* 1308–1316.

Ybarra, M. L., Mitchell, K. J., Wolak, J., & Finkelhor, D. (2006). Examining characteristics and associated distress related to internet harassment: Findings from the second youth internet safety survey. *Pediatrics, 118,* 1169–1177.

Cyber-victimization and popularity in early adolescence: Stability and predictive associations

Petra Gradinger[1], Dagmar Strohmeier[2], Eva Maria Schiller[3], Elisabeth Stefanek[1], and Christiane Spiel[1]

[1]Department of Economic Psychology, Educational Psychology & Evaluation, University of Vienna, Vienna, Austria
[2]School of Applied Health/Social Sciences, University of Applied Sciences, Upper Austria, Linz, Austria
[3]Department of Developmental Psychology, University of Münster, Münster, Germany

The present study examined: (1) the one-year stability of cyber-victimization; (2) the temporal sequence of cyber-victimization and traditional victimization; and (3) popularity and perceived popularity as possible antecedents and consequences of cyber-victimization and traditional victimization. The sample comprised 665 early adolescents (356 boys, 309 girls) aged 11.63 ($SD = 0.84$) at Time 1. Data were collected using self- and peer reports. To test for the temporal sequence a cross-lagged panel design was used. Traditional victimization, popularity and perceived popularity were moderately stable for both boys and girls. Cyber-victimization was neither stable during a one-year period, nor could it be predicted by traditional victimization, popularity or perceived popularity. Instead, cyber-victimization fostered popularity in girls. The implications of these findings are discussed.

Keywords: Cross-lagged panel design; Cyber-victimization; Early adolescence; Perceived popularity; Popularity; Victimization.

A growing body of evidence consistently shows that cyber-victimization co-occurs with traditional victimization (e.g., Gradinger, Strohmeier, & Spiel, 2009). However, because longitudinal studies on cyber-victimization are

Correspondence should be addressed to Petra Gradinger, Department of Economic Psychology, Educational Psychology & Evaluation, Faculty of Psychology, University of Vienna, Universitätsstrasse 7, 1010 Vienna, Austria. E-mail: petra.gradinger@univie.ac.at lacking, it is not known whether cyber-victimization and traditional victimization are similarly stable. Moreover, there is a lack of knowledge regarding the temporal sequence of the two constructs. It is unknown whether cyber-victimization mutually develops with traditional victimization, whether it is a consequence or an antecedent of traditional victimization.

Popularity in the peer group (e.g., having friends and being liked by peers) has been identified as one of the strongest (negative) correlates of traditional victimization both concurrently and longitudinally (Cook, Williams, Guerra, Kim, & Sadek, 2010). Concerning cyber-victimization the relationship with popularity is unclear. But it has been shown that a substantial number of cyber-victims are harassed in cyber space by peers known in real life (Juvonen & Gross, 2008; Kowalski & Limber, 2007; Slonje & Smith, 2008).

It was the intention of the present research to contribute to the knowledge on cyber-victimization by investigating the concurrent and longitudinal associations of cyber-victimization, traditional victimization, and popularity simultaneously.

Cyber-victimization and traditional victimization: Stability and temporal sequence

Although traditional victimization, by definition, implies a certain degree of chronicity and repetition (Olweus, 1991; Roland, 1989; Smith & Sharp, 1994), research focusing on its stability is rather sparse. Stability describes the consistency with which particular individuals are victimized by others over a particular period of time (Schäfer, Korn, Brodbeck, Wolke, & Schulz, 2005). The few available studies differ in their methodological approaches. For instance, samples were investigated ranging in age between 4 and 17 years; methods of data collection include self-assessment, peer and teacher nomination, and observation; and the intervals between measurement points range between three months and seven years. Traditional victimization appeared to be rather unstable in childhood (Kochenderfer & Ladd, 1996; Monks, Smith, & Swettenham, 2003; Wolke, Woods, & Samara, 2009) but moderately stable in preadolescence (Juvonen, Nishina, & Graham, 2000; Salmivalli, Lappalainen, & Lagerspetz, 1998; Smith, Talamelli, Cowie, Naylor, & Chauhan, 2004; Strohmeier, Wagner, Spiel, & von Eye, 2010). Furthermore, some studies found that victimization was more stable in boys compared with girls (Boulton & Smith, 1994; Camodeca, Goossens, Terwogt, & Schuengel, 2002) while other studies did not report any gender differences (Juvonen et al., 2000; Smith et al., 2004).

As pointed out by Dooley, Pyzalski, and Cross (2009), the criterion of repetition gets much more complex when considering cyber-victimization. On the one hand, one single negative action from a perpetrator might get uncontrollably repeated in cyber space (e.g., setting up a nasty webpage, which is watched by an unknown number of internet users). On the other hand, a cyber-victim might be able to stop certain kinds of repeated harassments in the cyber space easily (e.g., blocking a perpetrator on social network sites or chat rooms, or changing his/her identity in cyberspace). However, it is also possible that an anonymous perpetrator could repeatedly and uncontrollably harass a victim everywhere and every time without being identified. The question of stability is related to this issue. To the best of our knowledge, no study to date has ever investigated the stability of cyber-victimization. Because traditional victimization and cyber-victimization co-occur (Gradinger et al., 2009; Raskauskas & Stoltz, 2007) it might be the case that the two constructs show similar stabilities. However, according to the possibilities described above, cyber-victimization could be of higher ("everywhere and every time") or lower ("blocking or changing identity") stability than traditional victimization.

Beside their documented co-occurrence, nothing is known about the longitudinal relationship between cyber-victimization and traditional victimization. In principle, the concurrent associations might be due to three longitudinal patterns. First, it is possible that cyber-victimization represents an escalating "end" of traditional victimization. According to this hypothesis, traditional victimization would precede cyber-victimization because victims who have already been traditionally harassed would be followed up later by their perpetrators in the cyber space. Second, it might be that victimization "starts" in the cyber space and will then be followed up in real life. According to this hypothesis, victimization in cyber space would spread to real life. Third, it is possible that no longitudinal associations exist. This would indicate that cyber-victimization "spontaneously emerges" together with traditional victimization for only a short period of time. However, as it has been shown that a substantial amount of cyber-victims are harassed in cyber space by peers known in real life (Juvonen & Gross, 2008; Kowalski & Limber, 2007; Slonje & Smith, 2008), it is reasonable to expect that victimization could also start in real life and would spread to cyber space at a later level of escalation.

Victimization and popularity: Relations over time

Peer status has been identified as one of the strongest negative correlates of traditional victimization both concurrently and longitudinally (Cook et al., 2010; Hodges, Boivin, Vitaro, & Bukowski, 1999; Hodges & Perry, 1999; Perry, Kusel, & Perry, 1988; Salmivalli & Isaacs, 2005). Supporting a transactional model of development, it has been shown that peer status is both an antecedent and a consequence of traditional victimization (Salmivalli & Isaacs, 2005). Recent conceptualizations of peer status have assumed a model of two dimensions, one being popular and one being perceived popular (Cillessen, 2009). Popularity reflects being liked and accepted by peers, often operationalized through "best friend" nominations. Perceived popularity reflects high visibility and dominance in the peer group, often operationalized by nominations of "perceived as most popular". Concurrently, it has been shown that popularity and perceived popularity are distinct constructs, which are both protective factors for traditional victimization (De Bruyn, Cillessen, & Wissink, 2010). Cillessen and Mayeaux (2004) demonstrated a high one-year and a moderate five-year stability of the two constructs by applying a cross-lagged panel design. Perceived popularity was more stable than popularity, demonstrating a higher peer consensus for reputation compared with individual liking. Regarding gender, perceived popularity was more stable for girls and popularity was more stable for boys.

To the best of our knowledge, no study to date has investigated concurrent or longitudinal associations between these two peer status dimensions and cyber-victimization. Considering that a substantial number of cyber-victims are harassed in cyber space by peers known in real life (Juvonen & Gross, 2008; Kowalski & Limber, 2007; Slonje & Smith, 2008) it is conceivable to expect reciprocal associations between peer status and cyber-victimization.

It was the intention of the present study to provide knowledge about the stability of cyber-victimization and its relations to traditional victimization and popularity over time. Specifically, we examined: (1) the one-year stability of cyber-victimization; (2) the temporal sequence of cyber-victimization and traditional victimization; and (3) popularity and perceived popularity as potential antecedents and consequences of traditional victimization and cyber-victimization. We also explored whether gender would moderate these associations.

METHOD

Participants

Data were drawn from the untreated control group of an intervention study conducted in Austria (Spiel & Strohmeier, 2011). Data were collected twice in five Austrian schools (38 classes). In sum, data from 665 adolescents (356 boys, 309 girls), who participated on at least one occasion of measurement, were used for the present study. In May/June 2009 (Time 1), 447 adolescents (246 boys, 201 girls) aged 11.63 ($SD = 0.84$) years participated in the study. In May/June 2010 (Time 2), 589 adolescents (301 boys, 288 girls) aged 12.65 ($SD = 0.79$) years provided data. Complete data at both occasions of measurement were available from 371 adolescents (192 boys, 179 girls). Thus, there were two missing data patterns: Adolescents who participated in measurement 1 only (54 boys, 22 girls) and adolescents who participated in measurement 2 only (110 boys, 108 girls). To test whether the levels of traditional and cyber-victimization differed between these groups of participants, two multivariate analyses of variance (MANOVAs) were computed. Traditional and cyber-victimization measured at Time 1 were compared between Time 1 participants only and Time 1 and Time 2 participants, $F(2, 420) = 0.73$, $p = .48$. Traditional and cyber-victimization measured at Time 2 were compared between Time 2 participants only and Time 1 and Time 2 participants, $F(2, 575) = 0.29$, $p = .75$. These results suggest missing data patterns at random. Thus, full information maximum likelihood estimation (FIML) was used to include all available observations and avoid generalizability issues that could result from only using participants with complete data.

At the beginning of the present study (Time 1), 78% of the adolescents were born in Austria, while German was the first language for 47% of students. According to the official statistics of the Austrian Ministry of Education, in 2009 54.2% of the students attending compulsory schools in Vienna spoke a first language other than German (bm:ukk, 2010). Regarding socioeconomic status (SES), 3% of adolescents stated that their family would have less money compared with other families, 41% stated that their family would have as much money as other families, 10% said that their family would have more money compared with others, while 45% could not answer this question. Of the participants, 70% indicated that they used mobile phones and 40% stated that they used the internet several times a day, while 9% stated that they had never used either mobile phones or the internet.

Procedure

The procedure was in line with and approved by the local school council. Participation was voluntary and based on active parental consent. Participation rates were 55% at Time 1 and 73% at Time 2. Data were collected through internet-based questionnaires, which were completed during one regular school hour in the school's computer lab under the supervision of trained research assistants. The order of the items within scales was counterbalanced to avoid answering biases.

Measures

Cyber-victimization and traditional victimization

Both self-assessments and peer nominations were applied.

Self-assessments. Cyber-victimization was measured with one global and seven specific items ($\alpha = .86$).

1. Global: How often have you been insulted or hurt by receiving mean text messages, e-mails, videos or photos during the last two months?
2. Specific: How often have you been insulted or hurt by receiving mean ... during the last two months from other students? (calls, text

messages, e-mails, chat contributions, discussion board contributions, instant messages, videos or photos)

Traditional victimization was measured with three specific items ($\alpha = .68$), e.g., "How often have others insulted or hurt you by mean words during the last two months?" Beside verbal victimization, social and physical victimization were also measured.

The response format for the self-assessment items ranged from 0 (*never*), through 1 (*one or two times*), 2 (*two or three times a month*), 3 (*once a week*) to 4 (*nearly every day*) and covered the frequency of behaviours within the last two months.

Peer nominations. In the present study victim nominations originated from perpetrator perspectives and not from all class mates. This approach was chosen in accordance with Veenstra, Lindenberg, Munniksma, and Dijkstra (2010) to increase the reliability of the nominations. We asked adolescents who had stated that they had bullied others (a) verbally, (b) socially, (c) physically, or (d) in cyberspace by sending mean text messages, e-mails, videos or photos, to nominate the names of their victims. Adolescents were presented with class rosters containing all names of class mates and were allowed to choose up to five classmates from these rosters. In addition, they were allowed to refuse to answer or to state that the victim was not a class mate. Thus, self-identified perpetrators were presented with four items, e.g., "Who did you insult or hurt by mean words during the last two months?"

Peer nominations received by each adolescent were totalled and divided by the number of classmates doing the evaluations minus one (because self-nominations were not allowed), resulting in proportion scores ranging from 0.00 (*never nominated as victim*) to 1.00 (*nominated as victim by all possible classmates*) for each adolescent on each item. To capture peer-reported traditional victimization via one score the proportion scores of the three items (verbal, social, physical) were averaged ($\alpha = .60$).

Perpetrators in class

Self-identified victims were asked to indicate whether their perpetrators were class mates or not. These questions were asked separately for the three traditional forms of victimization (verbal, social and physical) and global cyber-victimization.

Popularity

A standard sociometric procedure was used to assess popularity. The adolescents were asked to choose, from a list of their classmates appearing on the computer screen, up to three classmates who were their best friends. The number of nominations received by each adolescent was divided by the number of peers in their respective classes doing the evaluations minus one (because self-nominations were not allowed), resulting in proportion scores ranging from 0.00 (*never nominated as friend*) to 1.00 (*nominated as friend by all possible classmates*).

Perceived popularity

The adolescents were asked to choose, from a list of their classmates appearing on the computer screen, up to three classmates they considered most popular in their class by asking them "Who is most liked in your class?" The number of nominations received by each adolescent was divided by the number of peers in their respective classes doing the nominations, resulting in proportion scores ranging from 0.00 (*never nominated as most liked in class*) to 1.00 (*nominated as most liked in class by all possible classmates*).

RESULTS

Descriptive statistics

The means, standard deviations and bivariate correlations of the study variables are presented in Table 1. Means for cyber-victimization using peer reports were very low. Nominations as cyber-victim ranged between zero and 11% representing zero to two absolute nominations per class. Means for traditional victimization using peer reports were also very low. Nominations as traditional victim ranged between zero and 33% representing zero to seven absolute nominations per class. To test for statistically significant differences between boys and girls, *t*-tests were conducted. Except for peer-rated traditional victimization, no mean level differences between boys and girls were found.

Perpetrators in class

Adolescents who identified themselves as victims of verbal, social, physical, and cyberbullying were asked to indicate whether their perpetrators were class mates or not. Seventy-six percent of verbal victims ($N = 194$), 79% of social victims ($N = 112$), 79% of physical victims ($N = 113$), and 62% of cyber-victims (N = 34) stated that their perpetrators were classmates.

Cross-lagged panel analyses

Longitudinal and concurrent associations were tested within a cross-lagged panel design using multiple group structural equation models (see Figure 1).

72

TABLE 1

Means, standard deviations and bivariate correlations between the study variables (Time 1) and stability (correlations Time 1–2)

Variables	Girls M (SD)	Boys M (SD)	T/df	1	2	3	4	5	6	7	8	9	10	11	12	13	14	15
Self-assessments																		
1. Cyber-vic. (global)	0.23 (0.69)	0.15 (0.52)	1.53/445	**.06**	.21	.47	.28	.35	.08	.24	.31	.20	.19	.20	-.04	.10	.07	.06
2. Cyber-vic. (call)	0.22 (0.62)	0.24 (0.74)	-0.21/424	.35	**-.03**	.30	.11	.21	-.01	.15	.08	.23	.09	.07	-.05	.07	-.04	.08
3. Cyber-vic. (text)	0.17 (0.51)	0.16 (0.63)	0.09/424	.24	.74	**.07**	.16	.39	.14	.10	.27	.31	.29	.14	-.04	.04	.10	.13
4. Cyber-vic. (e-mail)	0.10 (0.45)	0.13 (0.51)	-0.75/424	.10	.64	.68	**.05**	.54	.39	.69	.35	.20	.15	.32	-.03	.04	.03	.04
5. Cyber-vic. (chat)	0.11 (0.42)	0.17 (0.60)	-1.20/424	.13	.70	.78	.74	**.01**	.45	.52	.12	.23	.14	.18	.09	.03	.08	.02
6. Cyber-vic. (discuss)	0.08 (0.41)	0.13 (0.52)	-1.02/424	.16	.49	.60	.64	.73	**.08**	.26	.11	.09	.12	.11	.18	-.05	.05	.04
7. Cyber-vic. (instant)	0.16 (0.53)	0.20 (0.67)	-0.66/424	.05	.72	.76	.70	.83	.66	**.03**	.01	.20	.11	.19	-.04	.00	.10	.10
8. Cyber-vic. (photo)	0.10 (0.31)	0.12 (0.53)	-0.63/424	.31	.57	.44	.51	.51	.47	.57	**.26**	.20	.24	.19	-.04	.02	.11	.09
9. Trad. vic. (verbal)	1.07 (1.20)	0.89 (1.20)	1.62/445	.24	-.05	-.07	-.12	-.11	-.09	-.10	.03	**.43**	.45	.38	.13	.04	.01	-.12
10. Trad. vic. (social)	0.60 (1.00)	0.43 (0.91)	*1.81/445*	.17	-.04	.03	-.04	-.00	-.03	-.04	-.05	.66	**.41**	.20	.02	.07	-.08	-.19
11. Trad. vic. (physical)	0.43 (0.88)	0.49 (0.87)	-0.67/445	.21	.04	-.10	-.09	-.02	-.00	-.01	.04	.40	.34	**.20**	.05	.02	-.08	-.14
Peer nominations																		
12. Cyber-vic. (perp.)	0.00 (0.01)	0.00 (0.01)	-1.16/444	-.05	-.06	-.05	.08	-.05	-.04	-.02	-.04	-.04	-.07	-.02	**-.03**	.08	.05	-.05
13. Trad. vic. (perp.)	0.01 (0.02)	0.02 (0.04)	**-2.66/444**	-.02	-.05	-.07	.05	-.03	-.06	-.02	-.01	.17	.15	.12	.21	**.19**	-.05	-.06
14. Popularity	0.16 (0.12)	0.14 (0.11)	*1.92/444*	.08	.00	-.06	-.07	-.06	-.01	-.04	-.05	.27	-.27	-.15	-.06	-.16	**.50**	.37
15. Perc. popularity	0.12 (0.15)	0.12 (0.17)	-0.33/444	.11	.03	-.06	-.01	.02	.10	-.01	.00	-.14	-.18	-.11	-.06	-.15	.41	**.72**

Notes: N = 201 (girls); N = 246 (boys). Correlations above the axis are for girls, below for boys. For stability correlations see in the highlighted diagonal. Mean level differences and bivariate correlations which were statistically significant at p < .05 are indicated in **bold**, approaching significance in ***bold italic***.

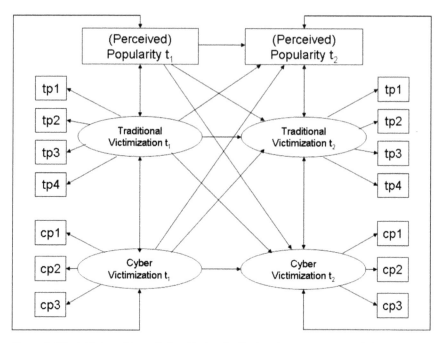

Figure 1. The initial model predicting the longitudinal and concurrent associations between (perceived) popularity, traditional victimization and cyber-victimization. *Notes*: tp = traditional parcels (1 = verbal, 2 = social, 3 = physical, 4 = mean of traditional peer nominations), cp = cyber parcels (1 = mean of global, call & text, 2 = mean of e-mail, chat, & discuss, 3 = mean of instant & photo).

The modelling was done using Mplus 5.0 (Muthen & Muthen, 2007). We implemented maximum likelihood estimation using the MLR estimator of Mplus, which provides standard errors and test statistics that are robust to non-normality of the data and to non-independence of observations. In addition, we controlled for the nested data structure on class level. Three criteria were used in evaluating the model fit: the chi-square test, the comparative fit index (*CFI*; Bentler, 1990), and the root mean squared error of approximation (*RMSEA*; Steiger, 1990).

Measurement model

In the first step, concurrent and longitudinal measurement models for traditional victimization and cyber-victimization were constructed. The latent factor traditional victimization was built using the three self-report items (verbal, social and physical) and the composite peer-report score. The model fits for both the concurrent (Time 1) model, $\chi^2(6) = 126.53$, $p < .01$, $CFI = 0.99$, $RMSEA = .01$, and the strict invariant longitudinal model (factor loadings, intercepts and errors equal of Time 1 and Time 2) were excellent, $\chi^2(30) = 40.24$, $p = .10$, $CFI = 0.98$, $RMSEA = .02$. Next, the latent factor cyber-victimization was built using the eight self-report items and the peer-report item. After excluding the peer-report item from the cyber-victimization measure, the model fits for the concurrent (Time 1) model, $\chi^2(20) = 159.48$, $p < .01$, $CFI = 0.91$, $RMSEA = .12$, and the strict invariant longitudinal model (factor loadings, intercepts and errors equal of Time 1 and Time 2) were adequate, $\chi^2(126) = 751.79$, $p < .01$, $CFI = 0.91$, $RMSEA = .09$. To yield an ideal just identifiable measurement structure of three indicators for each construct (Little, 1997), we parcelled the eight items by randomly averaging two or three items. Parcels are preferred for the consecutive analyses because, compared with items, parcels have superior psychometric quality that reduce both Type I and Type II sources of error but do not bias or otherwise inflate construct relations (see Little, 1997, for details). With parcelled self-report indicators and without peer nominations, the strict invariant longitudinal model (factor loadings, intercepts and errors equal of Time 1 and Time 2), $\chi^2(16) = 7.72$, $p = .96$, $CFI = 1.00$, $RMSEA = .00$, of the final cyber-victimization measure was excellent.

Structural model

We constructed two cross-lagged panel structural models to investigate the concurrent and longitudinal associations between traditional victimization, cyber-victimization and (perceived) popularity as shown in Figure 1. In Figure 2 only the significant paths for popularity and in Figure 3 only the significant paths for perceived popularity are displayed.

For popularity the model had an excellent fit, $\chi^2(91) = 177.33$, $p < .01$, $CFI = 0.96$, $RMSEA = .04$, using the whole sample. Because we assumed that gender would moderate the associations, we computed a multiple group model, $\chi^2(202) = 363.01$, $p < .01$, $CFI = 0.94$, $RMSEA = .05$, applying strong multiple group invariance (factor loadings and intercepts equal between boys and girls).

For traditional victimization, 50% of the variance was explained for girls and 42% for boys. For popularity, 27% of the variance was explained for girls and 28% for boys. For cyber-victimization, Model 1 did not explain any variance for either boys or girls. As shown in Figure 2, traditional victimization and popularity were moderately stable for both boys and girls ($0.44 < r < .64$). No stability was found for cyber-victimization (girls $r = .04$, boys $r = .00$). For boys, low popularity at Time 1 was a risk factor for traditional victimization at Time 2 ($r = -.16$), and traditional victimization at Time 1 was a risk factor for low popularity at Time 2 ($r = -.16$). For girls, cyber-victimization at Time 1 was positively related with popularity at Time 2 ($r = .22$).

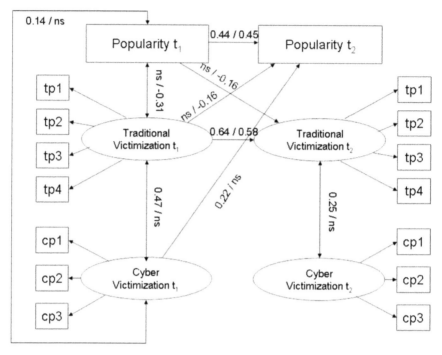

Figure 2. The final model for popularity, traditional victimization, and cyber-victimization. Significant standardized coefficients are shown for girls first, then for boys.

Second, we used a cross-lagged panel structural model to investigate the concurrent and longitudinal associations between traditional victimization, cyber-victimization and perceived popularity. Using the whole sample, the model had an excellent fit, $\chi^2(91) = 167.12$, $p < .01$, $CFI = 0.97$, $RMSEA = .04$. Because we assumed that gender would moderate the associations, we computed a multiple group model, $\chi^2(202) = 351.42$, $p < .01$, $CFI = 0.95$, $RMSEA = .05$ applying strong multiple group invariance (factor loadings and intercepts equal between boys and girls). For perceived popularity, 42% of the variance was explained for girls and 52% for boys. Model 2 showed exactly the same patterns of results as Model 1 and again did not explain any variance for cyber-victimization. Again, no stability was found for cyber-victimization (girls $r = .04$, boys $r = .02$; for further details see Figure 3).

DISCUSSION

This study investigated the one-year stability of cyber-victimization, the temporal sequence of cyber-victimization and traditional victimization, as

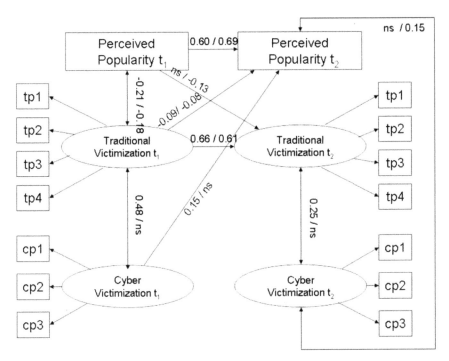

Figure 3. The final model for perceived popularity, traditional victimization, and cyber-victimization. Significant standardized coefficients are shown for girls first, then for boys.

well as popularity and perceived popularity as potential antecedents and consequences of cyber-victimization and traditional victimization.

The present study contributes to the existing literature in important ways. First of all, we detected that cyber-victimization is not stable during a one-year period although traditional victimization was moderately stable. This result indicates that cyber-victimization emerges rather spontaneously together with traditional victimization for only a limited period of time, as both constructs co-occur. A reason might be that cyber-victims are able to rather quickly stop perpetrators by, e.g., blocking them or by changing their own identity in the cyber space. Thus, a one-year period might be too long to detect an ongoing harassment in cyber space. On the other hand, it might be that a variable-oriented approach for data analysis is not able to detect a potentially very small number of stable cyber-victims (Strohmeier et al., 2010) as a high number of uninvolved students might inflate correlations between constructs. This is especially important for a rare behaviour such as cyberbullying or cyber-victimization. Therefore, it might also be worthwhile to look at stabilities with person-oriented methods for data analysis (von Eye & Gutiérrez Peña, 2004; von Eye, Mun, & Bogat, 2008).

Second, cyber-victimization neither predicted traditional victimization, nor could it be predicted by traditional victimization longitudinally, although the two constructs substantially co-occurred. This was an unexpected result given the high number of cyber-victims who stated that their perpetrators in cyber space were classmates. This result might again be attributed to the rather long time span (one year) investigated in the present study.

Third, cyber-victimization could neither be predicted longitudinally with popularity nor with perceived popularity. Interestingly, cyber-victimization longitudinally fostered (perceived) popularity in girls. A possible explanation of this result might be the developing romantic relationships between girls and boys especially in early adolescence, where the interest in relationships increases. It is possible that boys try to make contact with popular girls via mobile phones or on the internet and that these behaviours are perceived as cyber-victimization by these girls. It has already been suggested by prior research on bullying and victimization in early adolescents that boys who are bullies victimize girls (e.g., Craig, Pepler, Connolly, & Henderson, 2001). Of course, cross validations are necessary to prove this for cyber-victimization.

The present study also confirmed the transactional model of development in boys regarding traditional victimization and (perceived) popularity. For boys, low popularity is a risk factor for traditional victimization, and traditional victimization is a risk factor for low popularity longitudinally. For girls, we could not find similar transactional patterns as for boys. While popularity and traditional victimization were no risk factors for each other over the one-year period, only high traditional victimization was a risk factor for low perceived popularity longitudinally.

Concerning measurement, we used behavioural-based items to assess the various forms of the victimization concept. We did not use a definition of bullying (Olweus, 1991), containing the three criteria of hostile intention, repetition and negative power imbalance, because research has shown that victimization rates are lower when a standard definition of bullying is given (Vaillancourt et al., 2008). Also, given the very low frequency of cyber-victimization in Austria found in a prior study (Gradinger et al., 2009), we therefore did not provide a definition in the questionnaire. In addition, cyberbullying or victimization research shows considerable variability in definitions used, which neglects different criteria (see Tokunaga, 2010, for a review). The necessary criteria of cyberbullying or victimization are currently discussed in the scientific literature (e.g., Dooley et al., 2009).

Strengths and limitations

In addition to the longitudinal design, it is an asset that the present study (a) utilized both self- and peer ratings and (b) covered an exceptionally wide range of items to measure cyber-victimization. Furthermore, the use of a cross-lagged panel design allowed us to draw causal conclusions about associated factors of cyber-victimization for the first time. Our study is not without limitations, however. To begin with we did not randomly select our participants but we used a control group of an intervention study. For this reason teachers were not highly motivated to support the study. In combination with the need to use active parental consent this probably led to very low participation rates at Time 1. Second, peer nominations were collected from the perspective of victims and perpetrators and not from all class mates. Although this approach resulted in more reliable nominations, it also lead to a systematic underestimation of victims because not all perpetrators admit their behaviour.

Recommendations for future research

To understand the nature of cyber-victimization more accurately, long-itudinal studies with two measurement points are certainly not sufficient. Obviously, such designs are limited as they can only give first insights into the stability. To better understand unfolding processes over time, more measurement points with shorter intervals are needed and representative data should try to cross validate the results of the present study. In addition, it would be worthwhile to also consider other age groups and to use person-oriented methods for data analysis.

REFERENCES

Bentler, P. (1990). Comparative fit indexes in structural models. *Psychological Bulletin, 107,* 238–246.

bm:ukk. (2010). *SchülerInnen mit anderen Erstsprachen als Deutsch. Statistische Übersicht Schuljahre 2001/02 bis 2008/09* (Vol. 2/2010). Wien, Austria: Bundesministerium für Unterricht Kunst und Kultur, Abt. I/13a. Referat für Migration und Schule.

Boulton, M., & Smith, P. K. (1994). Bully/victim problems in middle-school children: Stability, self-perceived competence, peer perceptions and peer acceptance. *British Journal of Developmental Psychology, 12,* 315–329.

Camodeca, M., Goossens, F., Terwogt, M., & Schuengel, C. (2002). Bullying and victimization among school-age children: Stability and links to proactive and reactive aggression. *Social Development, 11,* 332–345.

Cillessen, A. H. (2009). Sociometric methods. In K. H. Rubin, W. M. Bukowski, & B. Laursen (Eds.), *Handbook of peer interactions, relationships and groups* (pp. 82–99). New York, NY: Guilford Press.

Cillessen, A. H., & Mayeaux, L. (2004). From censure to reinforcement: Developmental changes in the association between aggression and social status. *Child Development, 75,* 147–163.

Cook, C., Williams, K., Guerra, N., Kim, T., & Sadek, S. (2010). Predictors of bullying and victimization in childhood and adolescence: A meta-analytic investigation. *School Psychology Quarterly, 2,* 65–83.

Craig, W., Pepler, D., Connolly, J., & Henderson, K. (2001). Developmental context of peer harassment in early adolescence: The role of puberty and the peer group. In J. Juvonen & S. Graham (Eds.), *Peer harassment in school: The plight of the vulnerable and victimized* (pp. 242–262). New York, NY: Guilford Press.

De Bruyn, E. H., Cillessen, A. H., & Wissink, I. B. (2010). Associations of peer acceptance and perceived popularity with bullying and victimization in early adolescence. *The Journal of Early Adolescence, 30,* 543–566.

Dooley, J., Pyzalski, J., & Cross, D. (2009). Cyberbullying versus face-to-face bullying: A theoretical and conceptual review. *Zeitschrift für Psychologie/Journal of Psychology, 217,* 182–188.

Gradinger, P., Strohmeier, D., & Spiel, C. (2009). Traditional bullying and cyberbullying: Identification of risk groups for adjustment problems. *Zeitschrift für Psychologie/Journal of Psychology, 217,* 205–213.

Hodges, E., Boivin, M., Vitaro, F., & Bukowski, W. (1999). The power of friendship: Protection against an escalating cycle of peer victimization. *Developmental Psychology, 35,* 94–101.

Hodges, E., & Perry, D. (1999). Personal and interpersonal antecedents and consequences of victimization by peers. *Journal of Personality & Social Psychology, 76,* 677–685.

Juvonen, J., & Gross, E. (2008). Extending the school grounds? Bullying experiences in cyberspace. *Journal of School Health, 78,* 496–505.

Juvonen, J., Nishina, A., & Graham, S. (2000). Peer harassment, psychological adjustment, and school functioning in early adolescence. *Journal of Educational Psychology, 92,* 349–359.

Kochenderfer, B., & Ladd, G. (1996). Peer victimization: Cause or consequence of school maladjustment? *Child Development, 67,* 1305–1317.

Kowalski, R., & Limber, S. (2007). Electronic bullying among middle school students. *Journal of Adolescent Health, 41,* 22–30.

Little, T. D. (1997). Mean and covariance structures (MACS) analyses of cross-cultural-data: Practical and theoretical issues. *Multivariate Behavioural Research, 32,* 53–76.

Monks, C., Smith, P. K., & Swettenham, J. (2003). Aggressors, victims, and defenders in preschool: Peer, self-, and teacher reports. *Merrill-Palmer Quarterly, 49,* 453–469.

Muthen, L. K., & Muthen, B. O. (2007). *Mplus user's guide* (5th ed.). Los Angeles, CA: Muthen & Muthen.

Olweus, D. (1991). Bully/victim problems among schoolchildren: Basic facts and effects of a school based intervention program. In D. Pepler & K. Rubin (Eds.), *The development and treatment of childhood aggression* (pp. 411–448). Hillsdale, NJ: Lawrence Erlbaum Associates, Inc.

Perry, D., Kusel, S., & Perry, L. (1988). Victims of peer aggression. *Developmental Psychology, 24,* 807–814.

Raskauskas, J., & Stoltz, A. (2007). Involvement in traditional and electronic bullying among adolescents. *Developmental Psychology, 43,* 564–575.

Roland, E. (1989). A system oriented strategy against bullying. In E. Roland & E. Munthe (Eds.), *Bullying: An international perspective* (pp. 143–151). London, UK: David Fulton.

Salmivalli, C., & Isaacs, J. (2005). Prospective relations among victimization, rejection, friendlessness, and children's self- and peer-perceptions. *Child Development, 76,* 1161–1171.

Salmivalli, C., Lappalainen, M., & Lagerspetz, K. (1998). Stability and change of behavior in connection with bullying in schools: A two year follow-up. *Aggressive Behavior, 24,* 205–218.

Schäfer, M., Korn, S., Brodbeck, F., Wolke, D., & Schulz, H. (2005). Bullying roles in changing contexts: The stability of victim and bully roles from primary to secondary school. *International Journal of Behavioral Development, 29,* 323–335.

Slonje, R., & Smith, P. K. (2008). Cyberbullying: Another main type of bullying? *Scandinavian Journal of Psychology, 49,* 147–154.

Smith, P. K., & Sharp, S. (1994). *School bullying: Insights and perspectives*. London, UK: Routledge.

Smith, P. K., Talamelli, L., Cowie, H., Naylor, P., & Chauhan, P. (2004). Profiles of non-victims, escaped victims, continuing victims and new victims of school bullying. *British Journal of Educational Psychology, 74*, 565–581.

Spiel, C., & Strohmeier, D. (2011). National strategy for violence prevention in the Austrian public school system: Development and implementation. *International Journal of Behavioral Development, 35*, 412–418.

Steiger, J. (1990). Structural model evaluation and modification: An interval estimation approach. *Multivariate Behavioral Research, 25*, 173–180.

Strohmeier, D., Wagner, P., Spiel, C., & von Eye, A. (2010). Stability and constancy of bully victim behaviour—Looking at variables and persons. *Zeitschrift für Psychologie/Journal of Psychology, 218*, 185–193.

Tokunaga, R. (2010). Following you home from school: A critical review and synthesis of research on cyberbullying victimization. *Computers in Human Behavior, 26*, 277–287.

Vaillancourt, T., McDougall, P., Hymel, S., Krygsman, A., Miller, J., Stiver, K., & Davis, C. (2008). Bullying: Are researchers and children/youth talking about the same thing? *International Journal of Behavioral Development, 32*, 486–495.

Veenstra, R., Lindenberg, S., Munniksma, A., & Dijkstra, J. (2010). The complex relation between bullying, victimization, acceptance, and rejection: Giving special attention to status, affection, and sex differences. *Child Development, 81*, 480–486.

von Eye, A., & Gutiérrez Peña, E. (2004). Configural frequency analysis—The search for extreme cells. *Journal of Applied Statistics, 31*, 981–997.

von Eye, A., Mun, E. Y., & Bogat, G. A. (2008). Temporal patterns of variable relationships in person-oriented research: Longitudinal models of configural frequency analysis. *Developmental Psychology, 44*, 437–445.

Wolke, D., Woods, S., & Samara, M. (2009). Who escapes or remains a victim of bullying in primary school? *British Journal of Developmental Psychology, 27*, 835–851.

Processes of cyberbullying, and feelings of remorse by bullies: A pilot study

Robert Slonje[1], Peter K. Smith[1], and Ann Frisén[2]

[1]Department of Psychology, Goldsmiths, University of London, London, UK
[2]Department of Psychology, University of Gothenburg, Gothenburg, Sweden

We investigated cyberbullying in Swedish pupils, distribution processes of the bullying material, the role of actively targeted bystanders, and whether bullies feel more or less remorse when cyberbullying compared to bullying others via traditional means. Seven hundred fifty-nine children and adolescents (aged 9–16 years) participated. Cyberbullies not only targeted their victims, but quite often showed bullying material to other people they knew (39% of cases) and uploaded it onto the internet for others to see (16%). The actively targeted bystanders of cyberbullying mostly did nothing further to distribute the material (72% of cases). However, when they did distribute it further, they tended to help the victim by showing him/her what had been done (13%) more often than showing it to the victim in order to bully him/her further (6%); some others (9%) forwarded the material to other friends. Cyberbullies expressed less remorse than traditional bullies. Findings are discussed in relation to the definition of bullying, and the need for preventive strategies and for empathy raising awareness for cyberbullies.

Keywords: Bully; Cyberbullying; Internet; Mobile phone; Remorse; Victim.

After a decade of research into the phenomena of cyberbullying, various issues have been discussed such as prevalence rates (e.g., Raskauskas & Stoltz, 2007; Rivers & Noret, 2010), gender (Tokunaga, 2010) and age (Ybarra & Mitchell, 2004) differences, links between traditional bullying and cyberbullying (e.g., Gradinger, Strohmeier, & Spiel, 2009), impact (e.g., Ortega, Elipe, Mora-Merchan, Calmaestra, & Vega, 2009; Raskauskas, 2010; Smith et al., 2008) and predictors of cyberbullying behaviour (e.g., Williams & Guerra, 2007).

Correspondence should be addressed to Robert Slonje, Department of Psychology, Goldsmiths, University of London, New Cross, London SE14 6NW, UK.
E-mail: r.slonje@gmail.com

© 2012 Psychology Press, an imprint of the Taylor & Francis Group, an Informa business
http://www.psypress.com/edp   http://dx.doi.org/10.1080/17405629.2011.643670

Some features of traditional and cyberbullying can be quite similar, for example the type of behaviours, e.g., threatening or rumour spreading. However, differences exist between the two types as well (see Smith & Slonje, 2010), such as the 24/7 (that someone can be bullied at any and every time and/or place) aspect in cyberbullying, or the larger breadth of audience. Another difference is due to the nature of information and communication technologies (ICTs). That is, the bullying may more readily "snowball" out of the bully's initial control. However, although it may end outside the bully's control, it is not known if this was what was intended by the bully in the first place and/or by the persons who later continue distributing the material. No studies have to our knowledge studied this aspect.

This aspect of "snowballing" may relate to one criterion in the definition of bullying; that of repetition. The incidence of taking a photo/video clip once may well be regarded as repetitive behaviour if this clip or photo is either uploaded onto the internet where other people can see it later; or on the other hand, distributed among friends (Slonje & Smith, 2008). In the existing literature on cyberbullying prevalence rates, most studies have asked the victims and/or bullies how many times and/or for how long a period of time they have been cyberbullied (e.g., Li, 2006). However, due to the issues mentioned above, this may not be the best method of investigation as it is important to also consider the distribution process of the bullying material.

One important aspect of bullying research is that of intervention and prevention. Some of these programmes (e.g., Pikas, 1989; Robinson & Maines, 2007, Support Group Method) advocate that in order to successfully prevent bullying, the bully in some sense has to realize what she or he has done and/or feel some kind of empathy or remorse. However, no studies to our knowledge have been conducted within the cyberbullying context to investigate this issue. A few studies on relationships between empathy and traditional bullying have been conducted and, in a literature review of this topic, Hymel, Schonert-Reichl, Bonanno, Vaillancourt, and Henderson (2010) concluded that those children (boys in particular) who do bully express less affective and cognitive empathy. However, the authors do recognize that some aggressors can understand the point of view of others cognitively, but lack the emotional perspective. Jolliffe and Farrington (2011) found that cognitive empathy was not related to bullying on its own, however for males affective empathy was related, i.e., those males who had lower levels of affective empathy bullied more. Menesini et al. (2003) investigated moral emotions (including guilt and shame) in traditional bullying and found that to a higher extent bullies, compared to victims and outsiders, expressed "egocentric responsibility" "as a motive to justify the sense of guilt or shame" (p. 524). In addition, Muñoz, Qualter, and Padgett (2011) showed that even though someone may have empathy, if that someone does not care about the emotions of others, she or he is more likely to be involved in bullying others.

These issues may be a particularly important aspect within cyberbullying due to the anonymity of the bully or victim. That is, the cyberbully may be less inclined to feel remorse, guilt or shame compared to the traditional bully. For example, Zimbardo's (1969) "deindividuation theory" argued that if people were unable to identify another person, this would lead to less internalized controls such as shame or guilt. To draw parallels from this theory to the phenomenon of cyberbullying, often the cyberbully cannot see or hear the one they are targeting and in some instances they may not even know whom they are targeting, i.e., they do not identify their victim. This could therefore lead to fewer feelings of shame, guilt or remorse compared to a face-to-face interaction.

Aims

The two major aims of the study were: (1) to investigate the distribution processes of cyberbullying material in order to obtain a broader picture of how cyberbullying is taking place, i.e., how the material is used by both cyberbullies, and by those who receive it as bystanders; and (2) whether cyberbullies feel more or less remorse compared to traditional bullies. In addition we report on ICT usage, prevalence rates (for both traditional as well as cyberbullying), grade and gender differences and type of cyberbullying in our sample.

METHOD

Participants

Schools in the city of Gothenburg, Sweden, were approached randomly until nine different schools agreed to participate: two primary, two secondary, and five integrated (with pupils from both primary and secondary age). In each school two or three classes from each grade were randomly chosen. Of 789 students, one from primary school was not allowed to participate in the study by his/her parents, 15 from secondary school chose not to participate, and 14 (nine from secondary and five from primary) were excluded from the analyses due to very inconsistent answers or highly incomplete questionnaires. Hence the total number of participants came to 759: 243 students (115 boys, 128 girls) from grades 4–6 (commonly known as "*mellan-stadiet*" in Swedish, "middle-stage" in English) and 516 students (256 boys, 260 girls) from grades 7–9 ("*hög-stadiet*" in Swedish, "high-stage" in English). The mean age of the whole sample was 12.98 years ($SD = 1.55$); grades 4–6: 11.12 years ($SD = 0.91$) and grades 7–9: 13.85 years ($SD = 0.86$). The schools differed in terms of pupils' socioeconomic backgrounds. Some schools were in catchment areas with many families that were mostly native Swedish and/or had a good economy, while other catchment areas had many families from a variety of different nationalities and some in quite poor economic situations.

Questionnaires

The questionnaire was developed by the authors, partly following the Olweus Bully/Victim questionnaire, which has shown discriminant and construct validity (Solberg & Olweus, 2003). It gave the standard definition of bullying taken from the Olweus Bully/Victim questionnaire (Olweus, 1996). This definition includes the notion of repetition and power imbalance and also mentions that it is not bullying when "teasing is done in a friendly and playful way". It gives examples of different forms of bullying. It mentioned cyberbullying (*cybermobbning* in Swedish) as bullying through electronic means such as: mobile phone calls, text messaging, picture/video clip, e-mail, chatrooms, websites and instant messaging. The questionnaire was pilot tested on small groups of students to check for clarity and whether the students could understand what was asked of them.

The specific questions used for the current study can be seen in the appendix. The questionnaire used included other items as well on the nature of the bullying and emotions experienced, which are not relevant to the current study.

Procedure

Questionnaires were handed out to pupils in late autumn/early winter; two to three months after the term had started in 2007. This was done in their classroom or sometimes a larger room where pupils from two classes fitted together. The questionnaire took about 20 minutes to complete. Filling out of the questionnaires was supervised by the first author. The anonymity of the study was emphasized. It was stressed that no one at their school would have the opportunity to read any specific questionnaires. The pupils were also told that when they completed the questionnaire it would be collected and sealed in an envelope in front of them. Students agreed to participate informally; formal and written consent was given by each head teacher. Passive consent was also given by each pupil's parent(s), who had received all relevant information by post. Students were also advised that participation was optional, they were free not to answer the questionnaire as a whole, or any specific questions if they chose not to, and they could withdraw at any time (as mentioned above, five pupils did withdraw after this information, and 10 prior to this because their teachers had informed them of this option beforehand). This procedure was approved by the

Department of Psychology Ethical Committee at Goldsmiths, University of London.

RESULTS

Access to mobile phones and the internet

Initially pupils were asked whether they had their own mobile phone, and access to the internet at home. Mobiles were owned by 93.5% of the sample; 98.7% of the pupils reported having access to the internet. To analyse for grade (2 levels; 4–6 & 7–9) and gender differences a logistic regression was used on the categorical data. For mobiles, this showed a significant grade difference, $\chi^2(1) = 28.86$, $p < .001$, and also a significant gender difference, $\chi^2(1) = 12.23$, $p < .001$, indicating ownership by more older pupils (97.1%) compared to younger ones (86.8%), and more girls (96.4%) compared to boys (90.6%). No significant grade or gender differences were found for internet access.

Traditional bullying

When participants were asked if they had been traditionally bullied in any form, overall 15.8% stated they had been so in the last 2–3 months; 11.6% "once or twice", 4.2% more frequently. To analyse for grade and gender differences an analysis of variance (ANOVA) was used for the frequency data but showed no significance for grade or gender. Pupils were also asked whether they had traditionally bullied others; overall 15.0% reported having done so in the last 2–3 months; 11.8% "once or twice", 3.2% more frequently. A corresponding ANOVA using frequency data for bullies showed a significant effect of grade, $F(1, 751) = 14.15$, $p < .001$, older pupils bullied others more compared to their younger peers; see Table 1. No significant gender difference was found.

Being cyberbullied

Overall, 10.6% of pupils stated they had been cyberbullied at some point during the last 2–3 months (see Table 1); 7.6% "once or twice", 3.1% more frequently.

In the younger age group (grades 4–6), 7.9% of the participants had been cyberbullied; 5.4% "once or twice", 2.4% more frequently. An ANOVA of frequency data for victimization showed no gender or grade differences, however there was a trend for girls to be cyberbullied more compared to boys, see Table 1, $F(1, 748) = 3.31$, $p = .069$.

When looking at how the pupils had been cyberbullied the most prevalent form of being cyberbullied was by instant messaging (5.8%), followed by

TABLE 1
Frequencies of pupils who reported being victims or bullies (once or more)

	Victims of traditional bullying (N = 749)	Traditional bullies (N = 755)	Victims of cyberbullying (N = 752)	Cyber bullies (N = 758)
Grades 4–6				
Boys	13.2%	7.0%	5.3%	2.6%
	(N = 15)	(N = 8)	(N = 6)	(N = 3)
Girls	19.7%	9.5%	10.2%	3.1%
	(N = 24)	(N = 12)	(N = 13)	(N = 4)
Total	16.5%	8.3%	7.9%	2.9%
	(N = 39)	(N = 20)	(N = 19)	(N = 7)
Grades 7–9				
Boys	9.8%	21.2%	9.4%	12.9%
	(N = 25)	(N = 54)	(N = 24)	(N = 33)
Girls	20.9%	15.0%	14.5%	12.7%
	(N = 54)	(N = 39)	(N = 37)	(N = 33)
Total	15.4%	18.1%	11.9%	12.8%
	(N = 79)	(N = 93)	(N = 61)	(N = 66)
Total				
Boys	10.8%	16.8%	8.1%	9.7%
	(N = 40)	(N = 62)	(N = 30)	(N = 36)
Girls	20.5%	13.2%	13.1%	9.6%
	(N = 78)	(N = 51)	(N = 50)	(N = 37)
Total	15.8%	15.0%	10.6%	9.6%
	(N = 118)	(N = 113)	(N = 80)	(N = 73)

mobile phone calls (2.7%), text messages (2.5%), photo/video clip bullying (2.1%), websites (2.0%) and chatrooms (1.9%), with the least reported form being via e-mail (0.9%).

Cyberbullying others

Overall, 9.6% of the pupils reported cyberbullying others (see Table 1); 8.0% "once or twice", 1.6% more frequently. To analyse for grade and gender differences, again an ANOVA for the frequency data was used. This was significant for grade, $F(1, 754) = 29.41$, $p < .001$; grade 7–9 pupils were cyberbullying others more than their younger peers. For grades 4–6 the overall figure of cyberbullying others was 2.9%; all reported having done so "once or twice", none had done it more frequently. For grades 7–9; overall 12.8% reported cyberbullying others, 10.5% "once or twice", 2.4% more frequently. No effect was found for gender.

The most frequent form of cyberbullying others was by means of instant messaging (5.3%), followed by text messaging (2.6%), chatroom bullying

(2.1%), websites (2.0%), photo/video clip (1.8%), phone calls (1.6%) and finally e-mails (0.9%).

The distribution process of cyberbullying material

We investigated how the bullying material was used by the cyberbullies (see Question 9 in the appendix). Most cases (64.1%) of the 73 pupils who had cyberbullied others sent or showed the bullying material (e.g., a text message, a photo/video clip, etc.) to the victim they bullied. Quite often (39.1%) the bullies showed the material to their friends, and 15.6% reported uploading the material on internet for others to see, while 4.1% answered to the open-ended question that they had commented on pictures on a web page where others also may see what has been written.

A further question (see Question 10 in the appendix) asked how the material was used by those who receive it as bystanders. The 149 pupils who had been sent or shown such information had four different reply options.

Almost a fifth (19.8%) of the pupils reported that they had been actively targeted as bystanders. Of these, the majority (71.8%) did nothing with this information, hence ending the distribution of the bullying material further. However, 6.0% reported sending or showing the material to the victim in order to try to bully him/her further and 13.4% defended the victim by trying to make him/her aware of the situation. Also, 8.7% reported forwarding the material to other friends. For those who had sent/shown it to adults, the figures were: 0.7% to a parent (1 pupil); 0.7% to a member of school staff (1 pupil); or 0.7% to both parent and school staff (1 pupil). In 1.3% of cases (2 pupils) the pupils did not report to whom they had sent/forwarded the bullying material.

Do cyberbullies feel more or less remorse compared to traditional bullies?

Those pupils who had bullied others in either a traditional way or in a cyber way were asked whether at any point they had felt any remorse for doing so. Table 2 shows the percentages who felt remorse, first for traditional bullies (this will also include some cyberbullies), and then for cyberbullies (this will also include some traditional bullies; see Table 3). The majority (69.9%) of those who had traditionally bullied others did at some point feel remorse for doing so; a minority (30.1%) reported having no remorse. For those who had cyberbullied others the opposite can be seen; in the majority of cases (57.5%) the bullies had no remorse while a minority (42.5%) did. To analyse for grade and gender differences two logistic regressions were carried out; one for those who had traditionally bullied others with factors of grade and gender, and outcome variable of scores on remorse, and one for those who had cyber-bullied others. Girls generally felt more remorse compared to boys, which was

TABLE 2
Percentages of those pupils who had bullied others, who felt any remorse

Remorse	Gender	Traditional bullying (N = 113)			Cyberbullying (N = 73)		
		Grades 4–6	Grades 7–9	Total	Grades 4–6	Grades 7–9	Total
Yes							
	Boys	87.5%	55.6%	59.7%	66.7%	27.3%	30.6%
		(N = 7)	(N = 30)	(N = 37)	(N = 2)	(N = 9)	(N = 11)
	Girls	83.3%	82.1%	82.4%	50.0%	54.5%	54.1%
		(N = 10)	(N = 32)	(N = 42)	(N = 2)	(N = 18)	(N = 20)
	Total	85.0%	66.7%	69.9%	57.1%	40.9%	42.5%
		(N = 17)	(N = 62)	(N = 79)	(N = 4)	(N = 27)	(N = 31)
No							
	Boys	12.5%	44.4%	40.3%	33.3%	72.7%	69.4%
		(N = 1)	(N = 24)	(N = 25)	(N = 1)	(N = 24)	(N = 25)
	Girls	16.7%	17.9%	17.6%	50.0%	45.5%	45.9%
		(N = 2)	(N = 7)	(N = 9)	(N = 2)	(N = 15)	(N = 17)
	Total	15.0%	33.3%	30.1%	42.9%	59.1%	57.5%
		(N = 3)	(N = 31)	(N = 34)	(N = 3)	(N = 39)	(N = 42)

TABLE 3
Cross-tabulation between whether pupils feel remorse or not when either traditionally
bullying others or cyberbullying others

	If cyberbullied others have you felt remorse at any point?			
	Not cyberbullied others	Yes, at some point I have felt remorse	No, I have never felt remorse	Total
Not traditionally bullied others		13	15	28
If traditionally bullied others have you felt remorse at any point?				
Yes, at some point I have felt remorse	55	16	7	78
No, I have never felt remorse	13	1	20	34
Total				
	68	30	42	140

significant for both traditional bullying, $\chi^2(1) = 6.14$, $p = .013$, and cyberbullying, $\chi^2(1) = 4.07$, $p = .044$. No significant differences were found for age.

To investigate whether traditional bullies or cyberbullies show different levels of remorse after bullying someone else two other types of analysis were made; one chi-square for those pupils who either had only traditionally bullied others or only had cyberbullied others and one McNemar test for those pupils who had done both. Table 3 shows that 140 pupils had been engaged in some kind of bullying behaviour (as a bully). Of these, 68 (48.6%) pupils had traditionally bullied others but not cyberbullied, and 28 (20.0%) had cyberbullied others but not bullied traditionally. The rest, 44 (31.5%) pupils had both traditionally and cyberbullied others. One response was missing.

The McNemar test showed a trend ($p = .07$) for those who bully others by both means to feel more remorse when traditionally bullying others compared to when cyberbullying others. Table 3 also shows that in 16 (36.4%) cases out of these 44, pupils felt remorse when both traditionally and cyberbullying others. In 20 (45.5%) of the cases they did not feel remorse for either type of bullying. However, seven pupils (15.9%) felt remorse only when traditionally bullying others but not when cyberbullying and only one pupil (2.3%) felt remorse when cyberbullying others but not when doing so traditionally.

For pupils who only bully others by one type of bullying (either traditional or cyber) the chi-square showed a significant difference between the types of bullying, $\chi^2(1) = 11.40$, $p = .001$, in relation to remorse. For those who only had traditionally bullied others, 55 out of 68 (80.9%) felt remorse at some point while only 13 of the pupils (19.1%) did not feel remorse. For those who had only cyberbullied others 13 out of 28 (46.4%) did feel remorse at some point but the majority, 15 (53.6%) did not.

DISCUSSION

Being bullied was not infrequent; 15.8% reported having been targeted via traditional means, while 10.6% stated that they had been victims of cyberbullying, at least once or twice. No grade or gender differences were found for victims of traditional bullying. Cyberbullying victimization was less common compared to traditional victimization, which is in line with other studies (see Smith & Slonje, 2010; Tokunaga, 2010).

Cyberbullying others was also not infrequent, overall 9.6% of the sample reported having done so, at least once or twice. No gender differences were found, however a grade difference was shown indicating that the older pupils cyberbully others to a much higher extent compared to the younger students. In the younger grades (4–6) only 2.9% reported cyberbullying others. However, by grade 7 this figure was about 11% and highest for grades 8 and 9 (usually 14- to 15-year-olds), reaching about 14%. This large grade difference was not found among victims of cyberbullying, which could indicate that the older pupils are cyberbullying their younger peers.

One notion that has not been investigated thoroughly relates to the issue of repetition mentioned in the introduction and also to the notion of the bullying "snowballing" outside the bullies' initial control. This issue was investigated in two different ways. One was what the perpetrators actually do with the material (how they distribute the bullying material), and in two thirds of the cases they send or show it to the person they intend to bully. More than a third also indicated that they showed or sent the material to their friends, which could indicate that a repetition had occurred. First, they had perhaps cyberbullied someone (e.g., sent a nasty text message to the person) and then forwarded it to their friend(s). Quite a substantial number of pupils, around 16%, also reported that they had uploaded the material onto the internet for others to see. A minority (4%) answered to an open-ended question that they had written nasty comments on pictures of others on the internet, which could also arguably be counted as a repetitive act; at least so for the victims since the information is up there for them to see, if not for the bullies (however a repetitive bullying behaviour is occurring). As far as we know no other study has investigated repetition in this manner; most studies have been confined to asking either the victim or bully (or both) how many times (and over how long a period in some instances) they had bullied/been bullied.

The second way the current study investigated how the bullying material was distributed, and also the motive of the distributors, was by asking pupils if they had been shown or sent any type of information that was meant to cyberbully someone else and not them. These actively targeted bystanders were also asked what they did with the information. Almost a fifth of the pupils reported that they had been targeted with such material. Over 70% of these pupils did nothing with this material, hence ending the distribution, however a few (6.0%) reported sending or showing it to the victim in order to bully him/her even further. These bystanders had now become bullies as they were on one hand distributing the material further and on the other hand actively targeting the victim. On the positive side, about 13% defended the victim by making him/her aware of the situation (they stated they did this in order to help the victim), and these bystanders had now become defenders. The last results may be a bit harder to interpret; about 9% reported sending or forwarding the material to other friends and this could have been done either to bully the victim further (additionally distributing the material), or alternatively to involve another friend in order to help the victim. However, it was those actively targeted bystanders who sent/showed the material to a parent (1 pupil), a member of school staff (1 pupil), or both parent and school staff (1 pupil) who could arguably be most accurately categorized as defenders.

A limitation of the study was that no follow-up question was posed and the pupils did not indicate why they did this. It would be of interest to investigate this issue further in future studies. Another limitation is that although for some aspects (e.g., prevalence rates) the numbers of participants were sufficient, other aspects could have benefited from a higher number of participants (e.g., some cells in Table 3 are small). In addition only a single item question was posed in order to investigate the issue of remorse, future studies should try to include more than one item to investigate this variable in more depth. Future research investigating the issue of remorse including more participants would also benefit from using more advanced statistical methods (e.g., configural frequency analyses instead of McNemar).

It would also be of interest to conduct further studies on what bystanders, and especially actively targeted bystanders, actually do with the information in relation to different types of cyberbullying. This question arises due to the notion of "bystander apathy", as in the case of the public murder of "Kitty Genovese". Hunt (1993) hypothesized that since so many individuals were around the crime scene everyone assumed that someone else had already called the police. Although this was a very extreme case, it would be of interest to investigate if more bystanders tell someone else of what has happened in the private forms of cyberbullying, compared to the public forms where they may believe that others have already alerted either the victim or adults.

The question of whether pupils feel remorse or not after incidences of cyberbullying has to our knowledge not previously been investigated. The current study addressed this issue for both cyberbullying and traditional bullying. In traditional bullying the majority (70%) of pupils said they felt remorse at some point after bullying others, however less than half (42%) those who cyberbullied felt remorse. For those who had bullied others in both these manners there was a trend to feel more remorse when traditionally bullying others compared to cyberbullying others. But for those who had done either one or the other, there was a significant difference, in that those who traditionally bullied others felt more remorse compared to those who cyberbullied others.

Perhaps this difference arises because in cyberbullying one cannot see the reaction or consequences caused by one's behaviour. That is, perhaps in the traditional ways the bully does see the reaction or consequence and it may be that at times that is what the bully actually is after. However, at some point if this reaction or consequence is strong it may well be that the bully can feel remorse. But, when cyberbullying others often the bully and the victim are not face to face and hence even if the consequence is very strong, the bully might never know this and therefore not think so much about it, and thus not feel remorse.

This issue of remorse should be investigated further and at different levels in future studies. Some intervention programmes, e.g., the Pikas method (Pikas, 1989) or the Support Group Method (Robinson & Maines, 2007), acknowledge that it is of importance for the bully to feel empathy if the bullying is to decline or stop. It would be of interest to investigate what actually evokes the feeling of remorse in bullies. To start, future studies could perhaps compare all different types of bullying to one another to see whether the feeling of remorse differs between them and then perhaps carry on to study different levels of this feeling.

REFERENCES

Gradinger, P., Strohmeier, D., & Spiel, C. (2009). Traditional bullying and cyberbullying. *Zeitschrift für Psychologie/Journal of Psychology, 217*, 205–213.

Hunt, M. (1993). *The story of psychology.* New York, NY: Doubleday Dell.

Hymel, S., Schonert-Reichl, K. A., Bonanno, R. A., Vaillancourt, T., & Henderson, N. R. (2010). Bullying and morality: Understanding how good kids can behave badly. In S. R. Jimerson, S. M. Swearer, & D. L. Espelage (Eds.), *Handbook of bullying in schools: An international perspective* (pp. 101–118). New York, NY: Routledge.

Jolliffe, D., & Farrington, D. P. (2011). Is low empathy related to bullying after controlling for individual and social background variables? *Journal of Adolescence, 34*, 59–71.

Li, Q. (2006). Cyberbullying in schools: A research of gender differences. *School Psychology International, 27*, 157–170.

Menesini, E., Sanchez, V., Fonzi, A., Ortega, R., Costabile, A., & Feudo, G. L. (2003). Moral emotions and bullying: A cross-national comparison of differences between bullies, victims and outsiders. *Aggressive Behavior, 29*, 515–530.

Muñoz, L. C., Qualter, P., & Padgett, G. (2011). Empathy and bullying: Exploring the influence of callous-unemotional traits. *Child Psychiatry & Human Development, 42*, 183–196.

Olweus, D. (1996). *The Revised Olweus Bully/Victim Questionnaire* [Mimeo]. Bergen, Norway: Research Center for Health Promotion, University of Bergen.

Ortega, R., Elipe, P., Mora-Merchan, J. A., Calmaestra, J., & Vega, E. (2009). The emotional impact on victims of traditional bullying and cyberbullying: A study of Spanish adolescents. *Zeitschrift für Psychologie/Journal of Psychology, 217*, 197–204.

Pikas, A. (1989). A pure concept of mobbing gives the best results for treatment. *School Psychology International, 10*, 95–104.

Raskauskas, J. (2010). Text-bullying: Associations with traditional bullying and depression among New Zealand adolescents. *Journal of School Violence, 9*, 74–97.

Raskauskas, J., & Stoltz, A. D. (2007). Involvement in traditional and electronic bullying among adolescents. *Developmental Psychology, 43*, 564–575.

Rivers, I., & Noret, N. (2010). "I h8 u": Findings from a five-year study of text and email bullying. *British Educational Research Journal, 36*, 643–671.

Robinson, G., & Maines, B. (2007). *Bullying: A complete guide to the Support Group Method.* Bristol, UK: Lucky Duck Publishing.

Slonje, R. (2011). *The nature of cyberbullying in Swedish schools: Processes, feelings of remorse by bullies, impact on victims and age and gender differences.* Unpublished PhD thesis, Goldsmiths, University of London, UK.

Slonje, R., & Smith, P. K. (2008). Cyberbullying: Another main type of bullying? *Scandinavian Journal of Psychology, 49*, 147–154.

Smith, P. K., Mahdavi, J., Carvalho, M., Fisher, S., Russell, S., & Tippett, N. (2008). Cyberbullying: Its nature and impact in secondary school pupils. *Journal of Child Psychology and Psychiatry, 49*, 376–385.

Smith, P. K., & Slonje, R. (2010). Cyberbullying: The nature and extend of a new kind of bullying in and out of school. In S. R. Jimerson, S. M. Swearer, & D. L. Espelage (Eds.), *Handbook of bullying in schools: An international perspective* (pp. 249–262). New York, NY: Routledge.

Solberg, M., & Olweus, D. (2003). Prevalence estimation of school bullying with the Olweus Bully/Victim Questionnaire. *Aggressive Behaviour, 29*, 239–268.

Tokunaga, R. S. (2010). Following you home from school: A critical review and synthesis of research on cyberbullying victimization. *Computers in Human Behavior, 26*, 277–287.

Williams, K. R., & Guerra, N. G. (2007). Prevalence and predictors of internet bullying. *Journal of Adolescent Health, 41*, 14–21.

Ybarra, M. L., & Mitchell, K. J. (2004). Online aggressor/targets, aggressors, and targets: A comparison of associated youth characteristics. *Journal of Child Psychology and Psychiatry*, *45*, 1308–1316.

Zimbardo, P. G. (1969). The human choice: Individuation, reason, and order vs. deindividuation, impulse, and chaos. In W. J. Arnold & D. Levine (Eds.), *Nebraska symposium on motivation*. Lincoln, NE: University of Nebraska Press.

APPENDIX

The questions used and referred to in the text are given below. These are taken from a larger questionnaire, which can be consulted in Slonje (2011).

Class/Year: _____

Your age: _____

	Are you a boy or a girl?	☐ Boy ☐ Girl
	Do you own a mobile phone?	☐ Yes ☐ No
	Do you have internet access at home that you can use?	☐ Yes ☐ No
1.	First of all, have you been bullied in traditional ways in the last couple of months? Thinking of both at and outside school. (Not including cyberbullying.)	☐ No, I have not been traditionally bullied in the last couple of months. ☐ Yes, it has happened once or twice. ☐ Yes, 2 or 3 times per month. ☐ Yes, about once a week. ☐ Several times a week.
2.	Have you bullied others in traditional ways in the last couple of months? Thinking of both at and outside of school. (Not including cyberbullying.)	☐ No, I have not bullied others traditionally in the last couple of months. ☐ Yes, it has happened once or twice. ☐ Yes, 2 or 3 times per month. ☐ Yes, about once a week. ☐ Yes, several times a week.
3.	If you have bullied others in traditional ways in the last couple of months, did you at any point feel any kind of remorse?	☐ I have not bullied others traditionally the last couple of months. ☐ Yes, at some point I have felt remorse.

☐ No, I have not felt remorse
at any point.

4. Now thinking only of
cyberbullying, have you been
cyberbullied in the last couple of
months? (At or outside of school.)

☐ I have not been cyberbullied
in the last couple of months.
☐ Yes, it has happened once
or twice.
☐ Yes, 2 or 3 times per month.
☐ Yes, about once a week.
☐ Yes, several times per week.

The next two questions below are multiple-answer questions. That means
that you may tick more than one box if this describes your experiences.

5. If you have been cyberbullied in
the last couple of months, what
type of cyberbullying was it?

☐ I have not been cyberbullied
in the last couple of months.
☐ Through text messages.
☐ Through phone calls.
☐ Through photo/video clip.
☐ Through e-mails.
☐ Through chatrooms.
☐ Through instant messaging
(e.g., MSN).
☐ Through websites.
☐ Through any other way.
Please specify: _____

Now thinking of cyberbullying others:

6. Have you cyberbullied others in
the last couple of months? (Both
thinking of at and outside of
school.)

☐ No, I have not cyberbullied
others in the last couple of
months.
☐ Yes, it has happened once
or twice.
☐ Yes, 2 or 3 times per month.
☐ Yes, about once a week.
☐ Yes, several times per week.

7. If you have cyberbullied others in
the last couple of months, did you
at any point feel any kind of
remorse?

☐ I have not cyberbullied
others in the last couple of
months.
☐ Yes, at some point I have
felt remorse.
☐ No, I have not felt remorse
at any point.

The questions below are multiple-answer questions. That means that you may tick more than one box if this describes your experiences.

8. If you have cyberbullied others in the last couple of months, through what means did you bully them?

☐ I have not cyberbullied others in the last couple of months.
☐ Through text messages.
☐ Through phone calls.
☐ Through photo/video clip.
☐ Through e-mails.
☐ Through chatrooms.
☐ Through instant messaging (e.g., MSN).
☐ Through websites.
☐ Please specify: _____

9. If you have cyberbullied others in the last couple of months, how did you do it?

☐ I have not cyberbullied others in the last couple of months.
☐ I have shown/sent it to the person I have bullied.
☐ I have shown/sent it to other people I know.
☐ I have uploaded the picture/ e-mail/text, etc., on a web page on the internet.
☐ Through any other way. Please specify: _____

And now a different question.

10. Have you been shown or sent an act of cyberbullying that was meant to bully someone else? If so, what did you do with the information?

☐ I have not been shown or sent any such act.
☐ I did not do anything with the information I was shown.
☐ I sent/showed the information to the person who was being cyberbullied in an attempt to try to tease him/her.

☐ I sent/showed the information to the person who was being cyberbullied in an attempt to try to help him/her.

☐ I sent/showed or directed the information to one or more other persons I know.

☐ To whom (e.g., parent, friend, teacher) _____
_____

☐ Other. Please specify: ____
_____

How stressful is online victimization? Effects of victim's personality and properties of the incident

Frithjof Staude-Müller, Britta Hansen, and Melanie Voss

Department of Psychology, University of Kiel, Kiel, Germany

An online survey was used to assess the lifetime experiences of online victimization of internet users aged 10 to 50 years ($N = 9,760$). It gathered descriptions and categorizations of the most recent incident ($n = 4,498$), and analysed the variables associated with emotional distress. Results showed that less serious (verbal and sexual harassment, flaming) and more serious incidents (denigration, impersonation, outing, and trickery) can be distinguished. Both characteristics of the victims and properties of the incident were identified as predictors of distress. Higher neuroticism, chronic stress, and prior experiences of online victimization correlated with stronger stress. The safety measures of the provider, greater internet literacy, and, unexpectedly, offender anonymity correlated with lower stress. However, perceived distress depended most strongly on the impact on daily life.

Keywords: Bullying; Emotional distress; Internet; Online victimization; Personality.

Nowadays, many people use the internet to manage their social contacts both on and off the web as a matter of course. However, there are worries that especially adolescents expose themselves to the risk of negative experiences such as aggressive attacks (see Hasebrink, Livingstone, & Haddon, 2008). But those phenomena known as online harassment, online-mobbing, online victimization, or also cyberbullying, are not just a teenage but also an adult problem (Privitera & Campbell, 2009). Empirical studies on cyberbullying are based on more or less general definitions. Juvonen and

Correspondence should be addressed to Frithjof Staude-Müller, Department of Psychology, University of Kiel, Olshausenstrasse 75, D-24118 Kiel, Germany.
E-mail: staude-mueller@psychologie.uni-kiel.de

The authors gratefully thank Jonathan Harrow for translating the original German-language article.

Gross (2008), for example, define it as using the internet or digital communication to insult or threaten somebody. Others like Smith et al. (2008) draw more strongly on traditional definitions of bullying and describe cyberbullying as the aggressive use of modern information or communication technologies (internet, mobile telephone) to injure another, weaker person repeatedly, systematically, and over a long time. However, even though traditional bullying and cyberbullying overlap theoretically and in terms of victim groups, they differ markedly regarding certain properties.

First, information in the internet is permanent in nature. Data are easy to copy and distribute, the circle of potential recipients is vast, and compromising content is almost impossible to erase, so that a permanent, serious threat can emerge (see Kowalski, Limber, & Agatston, 2008). As a result, it is debatable whether the repetition characterizing traditional bullying is so crucial for cyberbullying (see Dooley, Pyzalski, & Cross, 2009).

Another characteristic of online communication is the perceived anonymity. It makes online victimization particularly threatening, by hindering victims from taking countermeasures to alleviate their situation (see David-Ferdon & Feldman Hertz, 2007). One-half of victims (40–55%) probably do not know the offender (Kowalski & Limber, 2007; Ybarra, Mitchell, Wolak, & Finkelhor, 2006), but estimates vary greatly (from 27% in Juvonen & Gross, 2008, to 69% in Ybarra & Mitchell, 2004). Although interviews with focus groups have suggested a relationship between distress and offender anonymity (Smith et al., 2008), empirical studies of the effects on the victims' distress have not been published.

Most studies on cyberbullying and online victimization have studied prevalences. Reported rates generally lie between 6% and 25%, although some studies report up to 72% for single cases of victimization (Juvonen & Gross, 2008). The very heterogeneous estimates are partly due to different definitions, operationalizations, and cut-off criteria. At times very high prevalence rates drop rapidly when stricter criteria are applied (Walrave & Heirman, 2011; Ybarra et al., 2006).

We view cyberbullying as a systematic, wilfully injurious use of information and communication technologies. However, many very stressful incidents can be found in which these criteria are either not met or cannot be ascertained. Therefore, we refer to online victimization as a broader category in which single elements of a definition may, but do not have to, apply. Thus, single aggressive acts via the internet are also covered.

Consequences of online victimization

Hawker and Boulton's (2000) meta-analysis has shown that offline bullying experiences correlate with various adaptation problems such as social withdrawal, increased anxiety, or depressive symptoms. Similarly, online victimization impedes psychological well-being as a social stressor (Ybarra, 2004). Beran and Li (2005) found repeated online victimizations in 23% of a survey of 432 7th- to 9th-graders. There were mild emotional effects (feeling angry, sad) in 36–57% of these victims, but severe impairments (feeling anxious, embarrassed, afraid, self-blaming, crying) in 15–19%. However, even more serious consequences have been documented: Cybervictims suffer more depressive symptoms than non-victims (Wang, Nansel, & Iannotti, 2011) and report slightly (but significantly) higher levels of thinking about and attempting suicide (Hinduja & Patchin, 2010).

Negative emotional reactions become more frequent when victimization is more intense and long-lasting (Ortega, Elipe, Mora-Merchán, Calmaestra, & Vega, 2009; Wang et al., 2011) or in the presence of additional problems such as simultaneous offline victimization (Gradinger, Strohmeier, & Spiel, 2009). However, alongside the unclear effect of an anonymous offender, there are other significant aspects of the modality of online aggression. Slonje and Smith (2008) found that college students considered online aggressions using *pictures or video clips* to be more serious than other forms. Staude-Müller, Bliesener, and Nowak (2009) have reported differential distress potentials for various types of victimization. Their survey of 1,277 teenagers revealed that insults and sexual harassments were less stressful for victims than the misuse of picture and video material or the disclosure of secrets and the threat of concrete injury. The boundary between virtual to real space is crossed when material from the real world (photographs, video clips, secrets) enters the internet or real injuries are threatened online (blackmail, incitement). Such effects on daily life were perceived as being particularly stressful. If the individual appraises the incident negatively, it triggers distress that then requires an adaptive response. Transactional stress models like that of Lazarus (1999) posit that this appraisal involves an interaction between stressor and person.

Internal and external predictors of distress

Within a broader concept of internet literacy, the appraisal of online victimization incidents may depend not only on the functional handling of digital media services (e.g., online applications) but also on the grasp of ethical standards (netiquette; see Shea, 1994; Stiller & LeBlanc, 2006) and the ability to handle online harassment effectively. Previous studies found that young persons with greater internet literacy in purely functional terms are exposed to more frequent risks (Livingstone, Bober, & Helsper, 2005; Vandoninck, d'Haenens, & Donoso, 2010). However, careful information management correlates with less victimization (Staude-Müller et al., 2009; Walrave & Heirman, 2011). Nonetheless, up to now, nothing is known about the influence of internet literacy on the appraisal of online victimizations. Victims who are more familiar with the medium and use it more intensively may well be confronted more frequently with online victimizations, but they may take them less seriously.

Online victimization takes place in virtual social networks, chatrooms, or instant messenger programs. The providers of such services try to counter the problem by employing moderators and operators who monitor their services, or by providing ways to report unacceptable behaviour in order to delete hurtful content or to sanction the aggressor. Research shows that victims are aware of these possibilities (according to Li, 2007, 70.5% of victims are aware of protective strategies) and also use them (Juvonen & Gross, 2008). Being aware of the existence of safety functions and considering them to be a low-threshold and effective response to cyberbullying may also serve as a resource that may also reduce stress.

The stress literature attributes an important role to the personality in the appraisal process (Bolger & Zuckerman, 1995). Neuroticism as a personality trait is defined as the ease and frequency with which a person gets upset and experiences negative emotions such as moodiness, anxiety, and depression. Persons with high neuroticism have difficulties in maintaining emotional balance, more frequently report problems in everyday life, and react to problems more strongly (Bolger & Schilling, 1991). Little is known about the part personality plays in the distress online victimization causes. The question arises if higher neuroticism makes the victim more vulnerable for negative emotional consequences.

Alongside internal variables, external factors also influence how a stressor will be perceived. Stress research has shown how the accumulation of external stressors contributes to increasing strain (Chida & Hamer, 2008). Further findings indicate that prior stress leads people to perceive critical life events (Green et al., 2000) as more severe. It is plausible that online victimization has more severe consequences when it is accompanied by other psychosocial stressors from everyday life. However, there are no findings on whether persons feeling overwhelmed by uncontrollable demands from everyday life have an increased vulnerability to being stressed by online victimization.

Research questions

Many internet users have negative experiences on the web. However, substantial victimizations that meet a stricter definition of cyberbullying are comparatively rare. Although highly negative emotional consequences of online victimization have been documented, little is known about what makes them stressful. The present study started by examining whether various types of cyberbullying differ in terms of the distress they elicit. It then examined the influence of different properties of the incident and the person on perceived distress. We anticipated that victimizations would be perceived as more stressful when the offender was anonymous or the victim had already experienced cyberbullying in the past. Incidents were expected to be particularly stressful when they impacted victims' daily lives. Finally, we expected that the awareness of protective functions in the cyber-environment would reduce stress.

For the characteristics of individuals, we expected that a high level of everyday stress and higher neuroticism scores would be accompanied by higher distress when online victimization was experienced. In contrast, we expected greater internet literacy to have a protective effect and to be accompanied by lower distress.

METHOD

We linked an online questionnaire to the websites of two German social networks (*SchülerVZ* and *Spin.de*) and informed schools about the link. The website received 32,365 visitors within four weeks. The great number of hits in the first few hours slowed down the data transfer, so that many users (13,128; 41%) gave up straight away. Others stopped working on the questionnaire while completing the first sociodemographic items (2,787, 21%). Data of respondents aged 10 to 50 were analysed and split into four groups (10–15 years, 16–25 years, 26–35 years, and 35–50 years). After testing responses for plausibility, we were left with data on the prevalence of the phenomenon from 9,760 respondents who answered the questions on demographics and prior online victimization completely (victimization sample). A total of 4,498 respondents gave additional information on a current incident and on their personality (distress sample).

Sample

The mean age of the victimization sample was 24.4 years ($SD = 9.05$) with 66.9% being aged between 10 and 25 years. The mean extent of internet use was 4.53 hours per day ($SD = 3.99$). At 68.8%, women were overrepresented in the sample.

The youngest member of the distress sample was 11 years old (10–25 years: 65.5%; 35–50: 15.2%). The mean age was 24.9 years ($SD = 9.11$). The extent of internet use was similar to the victimization sample ($M = 4.37$ h/day, $SD = 3.74$), and women were also overrepresented (75.7%).

Materials

The first part of the questionnaire gathered demographic information such as age, gender, and education level. This was followed by questions on prior and current online victimization, its consequences, and the respondent's personality. Table 1 reports descriptive statistics and the internal consistencies of the scales.

Online victimization. We assessed prior experiences with different types of online harassment with the seven categories proposed by Willard (2007) plus one additional "sexual harassment" category (see Table 2). Respondents were asked how frequently they had experienced such incidents on a 5-point scale ranging from *never* (1) across *once or twice* (2) *3 to 5 times* (3), *6 to 10 times* (4), up to *more than 10 times* (5). We assessed lifetime prevalence to get an indicator for the entire amount of experienced online victimizations that could be used as a predictor of actual distress.

Current incidents. Because the study focused on the consequences of victimization, we asked respondents to recall the most recent incident of online victimization and classify it to the eight victimization categories.

Stress. We assessed the emotional distress of this incident with 10 items on a 5-point scale ranging from *not at all true* (1) to *completely true* (5). The introductory phrase "How did you feel in the days following the incident?" was followed by items such as "It frightened me" or "I was depressed". Responses were averaged to form a scale score.

Properties of offence. We assessed the anonymity of the offender dichotomously with the item "Do you know the offender" ("yes" or "no"). We also used a dichotomous response format to assess whether the incident impacted daily life.

Safety measures of the provider. We asked whether the internet provider applied some sort of protective function on their website ("yes", "no",

TABLE 1
Internal consistencies of scales, descriptive statistics, and gender differences in the distress sample

	Items	α	Distress sample (n = 4,498) M (SD)	Men (n = 1,087) M (SD)	Women (n = 3,379) M (SD)
Everyday stress level[a]	6	.91	2.65 (1.12)	2.42 (1.10)	2.72 (1.11)
Neuroticism[a]	8	.84	2.84 (0.92)	2.58 (0.89)	2.92 (0.91)
Internet literacy[a]	14	.84	3.83 (0.68)	3.94 (0.74)	3.80 (0.65)
Emotional distress[a]	10	.85	1.79 (0.78)	1.64 (0.75)	1.83 (0.79)

Note: [a]Significant difference for gender.

TABLE 2

Items, distribution of types of victimization, and victimization properties in the distress sample

Category / Item	n	Effect on daily life %	Emotional Distress† M (SD)	Offender unknown %	Discussed with others (partners & friends) %
Less serious victimization	3,708	10.7[a]	1.72 (0.75)[b]	45.7[c]	60.1 (50.9)
Harassment — Somebody has insulted me repeatedly on the internet	918	15.8	1.78 (0.84)	30.6	64.1 (49.1)
Sexual harassment — I have been harassed sexually (e.g., somebody asked me intimate questions; sent me pornographic material)	2,586	9.0	1.71 (0.71)**	51.0	60.1 (52.6)
Flaming — Somebody gave nasty answers to my contributions to the internet	204	9.8	1.55 (0.67)**	46.6	42.6 (36.3)
More serious victimization	790	25.7[a]	2.08 (0.88)[b]	17.7[c]	73.4 (60.1)
Cyberstalking — I felt that somebody was stalking me on the internet	214	28.5	2.11 (0.87)**	22.0	74.3 (59.8)
Denigration — Somebody spread lies about me on the internet	154	22.0	1.93 (0.85)*	13.0	78.6 (64.3)
Impersonation — Somebody used my name on the internet and put me in a bad position (e.g., set up a profile and used it to spread rumours)	134	26.1	2.14 (0.90)**	24.6	73.9 (60.4)
Outing and trickery — Somebody has distributed embarrassing material about me on the internet (photos, videos)	148	21.6	2.11 (0.88)**	8.1	71.6 (57.4)
Exclusion — I have suffered social exclusion (e.g., excluded from a group, not wanted in a group)	140	27.9	2.12 (0.89)**	20.0	67.9 (58.6)
Total	4,498	13.4	1.79 (0.78)	40.8	62.5 (52.5)

Notes: †Range = 1–5. [a,b,c] Values with same indices differ at p < .001. *p < .05 for difference compared to total mean. **p < .01 for difference compared to total mean.

"don't know"). Responses were dichotomized by amalgamating "no" and "don't know" responses in order to indicate whether a person was aware of the function.

Everyday stress level. We assessed the degree of being overwhelmed by the demands of everyday life with six items taken from the German-language *Trierer Inventar zum chronischen Stress* (TICS; Schulz, Schlotz, & Becker, 2004). Respondents reported how often during the past three months they had been in situations such as "times in which everything is just too much for me" on a 5-point scale ranging from *never* (1) to *very often* (5).

Neuroticism. Respondents answered eight items taken from the neuroticism scale of the German adaptation of the NEO Personality Inventory (NEO-FFI; Borkenau & Ostendorf, 2008), for example, "I often feel tense or nervous," on a 5-point scale ranging from *not at all true* (1) to *completely true* (5).

Internet literacy. Two aspects of internet literacy were assessed and amalgamated into a sum score. Respondents first rated how confident they were about handling nine different internet applications (e.g., search engines, instant messengers, e-mail, social networks) on a 5-point scale ranging from *very unconfident* (1) to *very confident* (5). Five further items related to safety issues (e.g., "If people are harassed on the internet, there is somebody they can report it to.") and knowledge of netiquette (e.g., "There are rules for communication in the internet just like there are in everyday life").

RESULTS

In all, reports of prior victimization over the internet were very frequent, and the prevalence of the different types varied broadly (see Figure 1). Most frequent was verbal harassment, with 81.5% of respondents reporting at least one such incident. Sexual harassment was also very common (68.3%). More than one third (38.9%) of respondents felt that they had been stalked on the internet, and more than one half reported being exposed to flaming (53.4%) or denigration (53.3%). Impersonation (15.9%), outing and trickery (20.4%), and exclusion (22.1%) were less frequent.

Regarding age, data show that the lowest levels of verbal and sexual harassment, flaming, and cyberstalking were found in the youngest group of participants.

Gender differences were particularly strong for sexual harassment, $F(1, 9492) = 2788.5$, $p = .0005$, and cyberstalking, $F(1, 9442) = 120.8$, $p = .0005$, with female respondents being far more strongly exposed to both. They also reported more insults, $F(1, 9499) = 29.68$, $p = .0005$. Men, in contrast, were

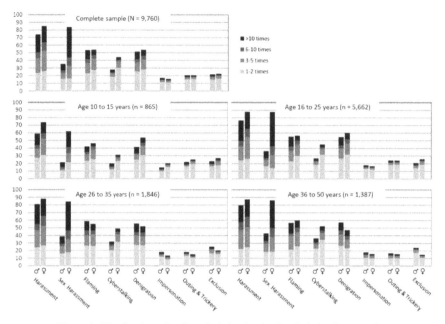

Figure 1. Distribution of online victimization in the victimization sample.

more strongly exposed to impersonation, $F(1, 9339) = 7.51$, $p = .006$, and flaming, $F(1, 9360) = 39.99$, $p = .0005$. Denigration, outing and trickery, and exclusion were equally prevalent for both genders, all $Fs \leq 1.291$, $ps \geq .256$.

One half of participants (50.2%) reported multiple victimizations, that is, experiences with more than three of the eight categories. This also differed significantly between women (55.7%) and men (38.3%), $\chi^2(1, n = 9121) = 151.54$, $p = .0005$. The rate was lowest among the youngest participants (40%) whereas it was highest in the group aged 16 to 25 years (53.4%).

The types of victimization also differed in current incidents (see Table 2). Once again, verbal and sexual harassment were most widespread. Relational aggressions (denigration, outing and trickery, exclusion, and impersonation) and cyberstalking were far less frequent. However, these less widespread forms were more emotionally distressing for victims and thus must be considered as more serious. The more widespread and mostly verbal victimizations, in contrast, triggered moderate or low stress. They can be regarded as the less serious types of victimization. Victims of more serious offences more frequently reported effects of the incident on their daily lives and that they knew the offender. Moreover, they had more frequently talked to others about the incident. However, these subgroups did not differ significantly in neuroticism scores, $F(1, 4496) = 0.164$, $p = .686$, internet literacy, $F(1, 4496) = 0.789$, $p = .374$, everyday stress level, $F(1, 4496) = 2.252$,

$p = .134$, or the extent of prior online victimization, $F(1, 4495) = 0.037$, $p = .848$.

We used hierarchic multiple regressions to test the role of the surveyed variables on perceived distress due to online victimization. We first entered the respondents' age and gender as control variables. Second, we entered the properties of the offence (anonymous offender, effects on everyday life) as dummy variables. In a third step, we entered internet literacy and prior experiences of online victimization. The fourth block was neuroticism and everyday stress level. Interaction terms were entered separately in a fifth step. Table 3 reports the results of the full model including the additional variance explained by each block (ΔR^2).

The regression explained 43% of the variance in emotional stress. Female victims and older victims felt more distressed by online victimizations. The age effect was even stronger in women. Gender was the only variable interacting significantly with age. Stronger distress was accompanied by higher neuroticism scores, a higher everyday stress level, and prior experiences of victimization. In contrast, higher internet literacy and provider safety measures had a protective effect. However, it was particularly interesting to see that distress was exceptionally high when victims reported that the incident influenced everyday life. Unexpectedly, the analyses also showed that it was more stressful for victims to know the offender.

Interaction effects are visualized in Figure 2. First of all, neuroticism and everyday stress potentiated the effects of one another. Moreover,

TABLE 3
Prediction of emotional distress by properties of the incident, internal and external determinants

Predictor	β	t	ΔR^2
Age	.093**	8.064	.022
Gender	.072**	6.186	
Anonymous offender	−.134**	−11.516	.300
Protective measures of provider	−.042**	−3.658	
Effects on daily life	.412**	34.208	
Extent of prior online victimization	.118**	9.811	.051
Internet literacy	−.121*	−10.249	
Neuroticism	.158**	10.935	.055
Everyday stress level	.125**	8.726	
Age × Gender[a]	.121**	2.100	.001
Neuroticism × Everday stress level[a]	.171**	2.940	.001
Neuroticism × Effects on daily life[a]	.206**	5.102	.003
Neuroticism × Internet literacy[a]	−.358**	−5.063	.003
Everday stress level × Internet literacy[a]	−.273**	−4.354	.002

Notes: $n = 4{,}609$; adj. $R^2 = .43$. **$p < .01$; *$p < .05$. [a]Interactions were analysed in separate regressions.

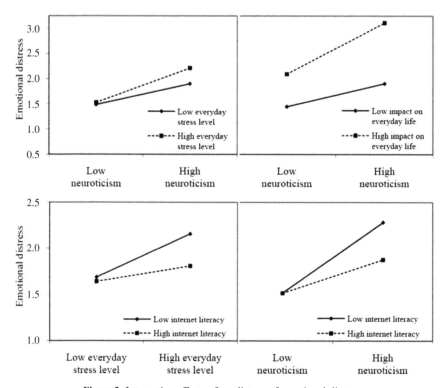

Figure 2. Interaction effects of predictors of emotional distress.

neuroticism had an even greater influence on emotional distress when there were real-life consequences. In contrast, everyday stress level and neuroticism had a lower impact when internet literacy was high.

DISCUSSION

Online victimization is a widespread phenomenon not just among the young. Although various prevalence studies have documented victimization in between one fifth and one quarter of respondents, the majority of respondents in the present study reported such negative experiences. Our victimization rates were probably far higher because they assessed the lifetime prevalence of online victimization. That may also be one reason why the youngest respondents reported least experience with the most common types of victimization. The high rate may also have been due to selective sampling and a sensitization to the topic through the survey context. Nonetheless, because the main purpose of the study was to analyse the determinants of stress, we were particularly interested in these cases.

First, it becomes clear that some types of victimization were accompanied by more distress than others. Relational aggression that attacks the victim's social network with defamation and slurs on reputation is more serious than verbal and sexual harassment. This supports earlier qualitative (Smith et al., 2008) and quantitative data (Staude-Müller et al., 2009) indicating that certain behaviours induce stronger distress.

As anticipated, characteristics of the victim are important for the emotional consequences of an online victimization. However, properties of the incident itself also impact on distress. Unexpectedly, our data rejected the assumption that offender anonymity is particularly stressful. Indeed, emotional distress was particularly high when the victim knew the offender. Although this contradicts the assumptions found in the literature (David-Ferdon & Feldman Hertz, 2007; Smith et al., 2008), it is, nonetheless, conceivable: Offenders in proximal social space may well intend more harm and have better opportunities to inflict it through better access to information, material, and the social network of the victim. In addition the victims might feel more betrayed when getting hurt by someone they know.

The proximity to the victims' lifeworld seems to be central, because the effects on everyday life are the decisive predictors of perceived distress in victims. This could also help to understand the relationship between age and distress caused by online victimization. It can be hypothesized that more damage can be done in the lives of people as they grow older. Hence, it is necessary to find ways to show users how to appraise these consequences realistically and to counter them. This is supported by our data showing that a high internet literacy and awareness of safety measures are accompanied by lower distress. A more precise understanding of these relationships will have to take account of the coping behaviour of victims. Although this was not included in this study, it is a central element in transactional stress models (e.g., Lazarus, 1999). The next step could be to study coping behaviour and its effectiveness.

Limitations

In this study we used a completely anonymous online survey that was freely distributed. Therefore we were unable to assure parental consent for young participants. Several limitations need to be considered when interpreting our results. First, the data are correlational. Although distress can be traced back to victimization because it is based on a concrete incident, our predictors were not assessed before the incident. The respondents' emotional instability and everyday stress may be an outcome of, for example, a decisive experience of online victimization. In addition, these are retrospective appraisals; current experiences may have distorted effects on daily life or the extent of earlier victimizations by making victims particularly aware of them. Such sensitization processes are also possible with the sample itself. Particularly strongly victimized or highly stressed persons may well be motivated to participate in such a victim survey. The high proportion of women, which is probably not just explained by higher victimization rates, also points to a degree of self-selection. Nonetheless, the very different frequency of less and more serious forms of victimization as well as the low level of emotional distress ($M = 1.79$ on scores ranging from 1–5) indicate that such selection processes had only a limited effect.

Conclusion

Our study contributes to broadening the perspective on online harassment and cyberbullying. Such widespread phenomena are particularly problematic when they become stressful for the victim. However, online victimization does not lead automatically to emotional stress. We have identified neuroticism and everyday stress level in particular as variables that increase the victim's vulnerability. However, if an incident moves beyond virtual space into daily life, then distress increases. That is the decisive variable.

Future research should examine these links between virtual and real space more closely. We now know that the majority of victims of more serious forms of victimization know the offender from other contexts, and that it is particularly the real effects on daily life that contribute to stress.

REFERENCES

Beran, T., & Li, Q. (2005). Cyber-harassment: A study of a new method for an old behavior. *Journal of Educational Computing Research, 32*(3), 265–277.

Bolger, N., & Schilling, E. (1991). Personality and the problems of everyday life: The role of neuroticism in exposure and reactivity to daily stressors. *Journal of Personality, 59*(3), 645–657.

Bolger, N., & Zuckerman, A. (1995). A framework for studying personality in the stress process. *Journal of Personality and Social Psychology, 69*(5), 890–902.

Borkenau, P., & Ostendorf, F. (2008). *NEO-Fünf-Faktoren-Inventar nach Costa und McCrae (NEO-FFI)* (2nd ed.) [German adaptation of Costa and McCrae's NEO-PI-R]. Göttingen, Germany: Hogrefe.

Chida, Y., & Hamer, M. (2008). Chronic psychosocial factors and acute physiological responses to laboratory-induced stress in healthy populations: A quantitative review of 30 years of investigations. *Psychological Bulletin, 134*(6), 829–885.

David-Ferdon, C., & Feldman Hertz, M. (2007). Electronic media, violence, and adolescents: An emerging public health problem. *Journal of Adolescent Health, 41*, 1–5.

Dooley, J., Pyzalski, J., & Cross, D. (2009). Cyberbullying and face-to-face bullying: Similarities and differences. *Zeitschrift für Psychologie/Journal of Psychology, 217*(4), 182–188.

Gradinger, P., Strohmeier, D., & Spiel, C. (2009). Traditional bullying and cyberbullying: Identification of risk groups for adjustment problems. *Zeitschrift für Psychologie/Journal of Psychology, 217*, 205–213.

Green, B., Goodman, L., Krupnick, J., Corcoran, C., Petty, R., Stockton, P., et al. (2000). Outcomes of single versus multiple trauma exposure in a screening sample. *Journal of Traumatic Stress, 13*(2), 271–286.

Hasebrink, U., Livingstone, S., & Haddon, L. (2008). *Comparing children's online opportunities and risks across Europe: Cross-national comparisons for EU Kids Online*. London, UK: EU Kids Online.

Hawker, D., & Boulton, M. (2000). Twenty years' research on peer victimization and psychological maladjustment: A meta-analytic review of cross-sectional studies. *Journal of Child Psychology and Psychiatry, 41*(4), 441–455.

Hinduja, S., & Patchin, J. (2010). Bullying, cyberbullying, and suicide. *Archives of Suicide Research, 14*, 206–221.

Juvonen, J., & Gross, E. (2008). Extending the school grounds? Bullying experiences in cyberspace. *Journal of School Health, 78*(9), 496–504.

Kowalski, R., & Limber, S. (2007). Electronic bullying among middle school students. *Journal of Adolescent Health, 41*, 22–30.

Kowalski, R., Limber, S., & Agatston, P. W. (2008). *Cyber bullying: Bullying in the digital age*. Malden, MA: Blackwell Publishing.

Lazarus, R. (1999). *Stress and emotion: A new synthesis*. New York, NY: Springer.

Li, Q. (2007). New bottle but old wine: A research of cyberbullying in schools. *Computers in Human Behavior, 23*, 1777–1791.

Livingstone, S., Bober, M., & Helsper, E. (2005). Internet literacy among children and young people. London, UK: LSE Report.

Ortega, R., Elipe, P., Mora-Merchán, J., Calmaestra, J., & Vega, E. (2009). The emotional impact on victims of traditional bullying and cyberbullying. A study of Spanish adolescents. *Zeitschrift für Psychologie/Journal of Psychology, 217*(4), 197–204.

Privitera, C., & Campbell, M. (2009). Cyberbullying: The new face of workplace bullying? *CyberPsychology & Behavior, 12*, 395–400.

Schulz, P., Schlotz, W., & Becker, P. (2004). *TICS: Trierer Inventar zum chronischen Stress* [Trier Chronic Stress Inventory]. Göttingen, Germany: Hogrefe.

Shea, V. (1994). *Netiquette*. San Rafael, CA, USA: Albion Books. (Retrieved from: http://www.albion.com/bookNetiquette/)

Slonje, R., & Smith, P. (2008). Cyberbullying: Another main type of bullying? *Scandinavian Journal of Psychology, 49*, 147–154.

Smith, P., Mahdavi, J., Carvalho, M., Fisher, S., Russell, S., & Tippett, N. (2008). Cyberbullying: Its nature and impact in secondary school pupils. *Journal of Child Psychology and Psychiatry, 49*(4), 376–385.

Staude-Müller, F., Bliesener, T., & Nowak, N. (2009). Cyberbullying und Opfererfahrungen von Kindern und Jugendlichen im Web 2.0 [Cyberbullying and children and adolescents' victimization experiences in Web 2.0]. *Kinder- und Jugendschutz in Wissenschaft und Praxis, 54*, 42–47.

Stiller, E., & LeBlanc, C. (2006). From computer literacy to cyber-literacy. *Journal of Computing Sciences in Colleges, 21*, 4–13.

Vandoninck, S., D'Haenens, L., & Donoso, V. (2010). Digital literacy of Flemish youth: How do they handle online content risks? *Communications, 35*, 397–416.

Walrave, M., & Heirman, W. (2011). Cyberbullying: Predicting victimization and perpetration. *Children & Society, 25*(1), 59–72.

Wang, J., Nansel, T., & Iannotti, R. (2011). Cyber and traditional bullying: Differential association with depression. *Journal of Adolescent Health, 48*, 415–417.

Willard, N. (2007). *Cyberbullying and cyberthreats: Responding to the challenge of online social cruelty, threats, and distress*. Champaign, IL: Research Press.

Ybarra, M. (2004). Linkages between depressive symptomatology and internet harassment among young regular internet users. *Cyberpsychology & Behavior, 7,* 247–257.

Ybarra, M., & Mitchell, K. (2004). Youth engaging in online harassment: Associations with caregiver–child relationships, internet use, and personal characteristics. *Journal of Adolescence, 27,* 319–336.

Ybarra, M., Mitchell, K., Wolak, J., & Finkelhor, D. (2006). Examining characteristics and associated distress related to internet harassment: Findings from the Second Youth Internet Safety Survey. *Pediatrics, 188,* 1169–1177.

The association between the mental health and behavioural problems of students and their reactions to cyber-victimization

Julian J. Dooley[1], Therese Shaw[2], and Donna Cross[2]

[1]School of Law and Justice, Edith Cowan University, Joondalup, WA, Australia
[2]School of Exercise, Biomedical and Health Sciences, Edith Cowan University, Mt Lawley, WA, Australia

Cyber-victimization is associated with mental health and behavioural problems and, consequently, young people need effective coping strategies. This study examined the relationship between the aggressive, assertive and passive actions of students after cyber-victimization and their mental health and behavioural problems. In total, 472 students reported being cyber-victimized (primary $n = 101$, secondary $n = 371$) and taking action. Student actions did not predict depressive or emotional symptoms. Students who responded aggressively used significantly fewer assertive strategies, had more conduct and hyperactivity problems, more overall difficulties, and fewer prosocial behaviours than students who responded assertively but not aggressively. Primary students reported more emotional symptoms and peer problems than secondary students. This study has important implications for the type (e.g., prosocial ICT skills, assertive skills training) and timing of the support provided to students who are cyber-victimized.

Keywords: Cyber-victimization; Coping; Mental health; Social problem-solving.

Correspondence should be addressed to Julian Dooley, Sellenger Centre for Research in Law, Justice and Social Change, School of Law and Justice, Edith Cowan University, 270 Joondalup Dr., Joondalup, WA 6027, Australia. E-mail: j.dooley@ecu.edu.au

The *Cyber Friendly Project (PEET)* from which these data were taken was funded by the West Australian Department of Education, Public Education Endowment Trust.

We would also like to acknowledge the work of Melanie Epstein, Debora Brown and Mitch Read for their contribution to this study.

http://www.psypress.com/edp   http://dx.doi.org/10.1080/17405629.2011.648425

Cyberbullying has been defined as "when, over a period of time, an individual or group use Information and Communication Technologies (ICT) to intentionally harm a person, who finds it hard to stop this bullying continuing" (Child Health Promotion Research Centre, 2010). Despite the intense scrutiny and discussion, there remains much to learn about the nature and impact of cyberbullying (Dooley, Pzyalski, & Cross, 2009; Rivers & Noret, 2010).

Nonetheless, growing evidence highlights the negative impact of cyber-victimization (i.e., being cyberbullied) on mental, emotional, physical and social functioning. For example, cross-sectional studies have demonstrated that being cyber-victimized was associated with depression (Perren, Dooley, Shaw, & Cross, 2010; Wang, Nansel, & Iannotti, 2011), conduct and emotional problems (Dooley, Gradinger, Strohmeier, Cross, & Spiel, 2010; Gradinger, Strohmeier, & Spiel, 2009), not feeling safe at school (Cross et al., 2009; Sourander et al., 2010), physical pain, frequent smoking and misuse of alcohol (Sourander et al., 2010).

Furthermore, cyber-victimized students (compared to those victimized offline) are less likely to talk to an adult suggesting that they may be more likely to try to manage the bullying on their own or in consultation with peers (Dooley et al., 2010; Smith et al., 2008). Therefore, the social problem solving (SPS) skills that students possess become critical to the successful resolution of the bullying incident.

We were unable to find any studies describing student actions in response to cyber-victimization. However, Camodeca and Goossens (2005) reported that students who were victimized (non-cyber) indicated they would most commonly retaliate (i.e., fight back), get support from peers or adults or ignore the attack; actions that can be considered aggressive, assertive and passive, respectively. Consistently, Black, Weinles, and Washington (2010) reported that students who were victimized most commonly fought back (63%), ignored (52%), told an adult at home (44%), or a peer (42%).

A key question in relation to post-victimization actions is the reason why individuals respond the way they do. Using a stress–coping model, Cassidy and Taylor (2005) suggested that young people who are victimized are more likely to exhibit psychological ill health if they use ineffective coping strategies (i.e., aggression) or feel unsupported during the experience. An important element of coping is problem-solving style, a pattern of cognitive functioning, which has a significant influence on how people respond to social problems and deal with life stress. SPS skills have been linked with aggressive (e.g., Crick & Dodge, 1999) and bullying behaviours (e.g., Warden & MacKinnon, 2003).

An example of ineffective coping (and poor SPS skills) is the use of inappropriate behaviours, such as aggression or bullying. Conversely, good or positive coping would include assertive or prosocial ways of dealing with interpersonal problems. Consistently, it has been demonstrated that bully victims (i.e., those who are bullied and bully others) have the lowest levels of SPS, the highest levels of psychological distress, externalizing and internalizing problems when compared to students who bullied only, were victimized only or were not involved (e.g., Cassidy & Taylor, 2005; Haynie et al., 2001; Menesini, Modena, & Tani, 2009). Importantly, Cassidy (2009) also suggested that passive strategies (e.g., failing to talk or avoiding) should be considered an example of negative coping and poor SPS.

Developmental issues

The impact of development on SPS is important to consider. It has long been known that older children generate more responses to social problems than younger children (e.g., Feldman & Dodge, 1987). The SPS skills of older children are generally more effective and appropriate than those of younger children (Mayeux & Cillessen, 2003; Takahashi, Koseki, & Shimada, 2009); younger children use passive strategies (e.g., ignoring) more often (Camodeca & Goossens, 2005).

In general, SPS skills improve with age such that by adulthood problem-solving skills mediate the link between stress and psychological wellbeing (Chang, D'Zurilla, & Sanna, 2009); the better the problem-solving skills, the better the psychological wellbeing after stress. Thus, in the absence of negative experiences (e.g., victimization), good or positive coping skills should develop with age. Interestingly, improvements in SPS have been linked with a hypothesized developmental shift in sociocognitive functions between the ages of 6 and 8 (e.g., Lively & Bromley, 1973; Yeates & Selman, 1989). Improvements in SPS may explain why older children typically generate more socially appropriate and less aggressive responses to social problems.

Thus, we were interested in examining the relationship between students' reactions to cyber-victimization and associated mental-health and behavioural symptoms. The aim of this study was to determine if the type of action a student reported engaging in after being cyber-victimized was associated with self-reported mental health (i.e., depression) and behaviour problems. It was hypothesized that post-victimization aggression would be associated with poorer self-reported mental health and more behaviour problems and assertive actions with better mental health outcomes and fewer behaviour problems. Further, it was hypothesized that passive actions (e.g., ignoring or doing nothing) would be associated with poorer mental health and more behaviour problems than assertive actions. Finally, it was hypothesized that secondary-school students would use more assertive actions in response to cyber-victimization than would primary-school students.

METHOD

Participants

These data were collected in 2008 as part of a larger study, the *Cyber Friendly Project* (Cross, Brown, Epstein, & Shaw, 2010), which involved 2,645 students from seven primary ($n = 682$) and six secondary ($n = 1963$) non-government schools in Western Australia, comprising seven metropolitan and six non-metropolitan schools (based on stratified random sampling). As we were interested in students who reported being cyber-victimized, our subsample of interest included 516 students (primary $n = 111$, secondary $n = 405$). Of these, 91% ($n = 472$, primary $n = 101$, secondary $n = 371$) responded to the questions related to taking some action as a result of the cyber-victimization (the remaining 9% were excluded because the action they reported could not be classified). Of this, 30% were male ($n = 133$; female $n = 315$) and 49% lived in the metropolitan area ($n = 233$; non-metropolitan $n = 239$). Primary students were in Grades 5–7 (range 10–12 years, mean age = 11 years, $SD = 0.77$ years) and secondary students in Grades 8–10 (range 12–16 years, mean age = 13.8 years, $SD = 0.90$ years).

Measures

Cyber-victimization. The 8-item Cyber-Victimization Scale measured participants' self-reported experiences with cyber-victimization. Participants indicated on a 5-point Likert scale how often they experienced each of these behaviours, which included being sent nasty e-mails or nasty messages on the internet, having mean or nasty comments posted on websites (e.g., MySpace or Facebook), or being left out or ignored over the internet. Their responses ranged from "*Never*" to "*Most days this term*". Cronbach's alpha for the total sample in this study for the cyber-victimization scale was .87. A mean score (range 1–5) of the eight items was calculated and included in the analyses as a measure of the level of cyber-victimization experienced.

Mental health. Mental health was assessed using the Depression, Anxiety and Stress Scale (DASS; Lovibond & Lovibond, 1995). Responses range from 0 "*Does not apply to me*" to 3 "*Most of the time*". The 14 DASS depression items were used to calculate a sum score (range 0–42) and the natural log of the sum score plus one taken (range 0–3.76) to reduce skew. Cronbach's alpha for the total sample on the DASS was .96.

Behavioural functioning. Behaviour problems were assessed using the Strengths and Difficulties Questionnaire (SDQ; Goodman, 2001). The SDQ provides a total difficulties score and five subscale scores—emotional symptoms, conduct problems, hyperactivity, peer problems and prosocial behaviours—with responses ranging from 0 *"Not true"* to 2 *"Certainly true"*. Cronbach's alpha for the total sample in this study were: total difficulties $= .80$, emotional symptoms $= .70$, conduct problems $= .63$, hyperactivity $= .69$, peer problems $= .56$ and prosocial behaviours $= .70$. Sum scores were calculated for each subscale (range 0–10) and total difficulties (range 0–40).

Actions. Using an index listing thirteen different actions, participants indicated which they took if cyber-victimized during the school year the data were collected (i.e., Terms 1 & 2, 2008), usually the previous six months. Multiple responses were possible as students may have been cyber-victimized on a number of occasions and have chosen to respond in more than one way each time. Two actions were excluded as they were considered an emotional response (e.g., felt sad or cried) and two actions were excluded as categorization was not clear (e.g., kept printed record of messages, turned off computer). Consistent with Camodeca and Goossens (2005), the remaining items were categorized into aggressive (1 item; i.e., sent nasty words or pictures back), assertive (4 items; e.g., made a joke of it, told a parent or teacher), or passive actions (4 items; e.g., did nothing, did not respond to messages). While students could have reported using any combination of these types of actions, they were categorized into one of three mutually exclusive groups, namely those whose response was:

- *aggressive* (may have also been passive AND/OR assertive);
- *assertive* (and also possibly passive but NOT aggressive); or
- *passive* only (and NOT assertive or aggressive).

Importantly, given the need to focus on the implications of engaging in an aggressive action post-victimization, participants were included in the aggressive action group if they responded affirmatively to this item. Participants in this group could also have engaged in assertive and/or passive actions, but the defining characteristic is their reported use of an aggressive behaviour. Participants were included in the assertive group if they responded affirmatively to any of the assertive items but not the aggressive item. While they may also have reacted passively, this group took assertive but not aggressive action. Finally, participants were included in the passive group if they only responded to the passive items.

Procedure

Data were collected from students by school staff within each classroom (according to a strict procedural protocol) at the end of the second term at school (June/July) and the beginning of Term 3 (July/August), 2008. The survey was read aloud to the Grade 5 and 6 students whereas students in Grades 7–10 self-administered their surveys. An active–passive parent consent process was used where parents were first asked on several occasions to return their signed consent form and then non-responding parents were asked to indicate their non-consent to their child participating. Eighty-five percent of students had parental consent (active or passive) to participate. Those without consent (either type) were given an alternative activity. Student surveys were collected by the classroom teacher and returned to the research team. The University Human Research Ethics Committee and relevant school authorities approved this study.

Data analyses

Associations between each of the mental-health outcomes and actions taken were tested in Stata 10 using random effects models, one for each dependent variable. Random intercepts were included in the models to account for school-level clustering. School level (primary/secondary) was included in each model as a factor and, importantly, level of cyber-victimization as a covariate to control and account for the impact of frequent experiences of victimization. Gender was also included in the models to account for confounding effects (gender was correlated with both the actions taken and the outcome variables) and so more accurately estimate the differences in mental health and behavioural outcomes for the different action groups. As gender was not a focus of these analyses the gender figures are not presented. The significance of the multi-category actions variable was tested using a likelihood-ratio chi-squared test of the variable's contribution to each model. Each model was re-run to obtain all pairwise comparisons of the three action groups.

RESULTS

The majority of cyber-victimized students (85%) took more than one action, with 21% reporting two, 24% reporting three and 40% reporting four or more actions (see Table 1 for detailed results).

Action group characteristics

A minority of the sample (13%) reported a passive response only and comprise the passive action group (Table 2). A third to a half of the students' action responses were aggressive (35%) or assertive (52%). As students may have experienced cyber-victimization on multiple occasions and may have responded in more than one way, some overlap exists in the

TABLE 1
Actions taken by students after being cyber-victimized

Action[†]	n	%
Passive responses		
Did nothing	140	30
Ignored the student bullying them	284	61
Did not respond	196	42
Stayed away from website where bullying occurred	102	22
Assertive responses		
Told the student to stop	235	50
Made a joke of it	157	34
Changed phone number, password, got a silent number	93	20
Told a parent or teacher	179	39
Aggressive response		
Sent nasty words or pictures back to person	167	36

Note: [†]Students may have endorsed more than one action as they may have been cyber-victimized on more than one occasion and may have chosen more than one action when victimized.

TABLE 2
Frequencies of students in "action taken" groups

Action taken after cyber-victimization			*Assertive group*		*Aggressive group*			
			Assertive only	*Assertive and passive*	*Aggressive only*	*Aggressive & assertive*	*Aggressive & passive*	*Aggressive, assertive & passive*
Group 1:	n	62						
Passive	(%)	(13)						
Group 2:	n	243	50	193				
Assertive	(%)	(52)	(21)	(79)				
Group 3:	n	167			15	27	24	101
Aggressive	(%)	(35)			(9)	(16)	(14)	(61)
Total	n	472						
	(%)	(100)						

actions reported by the three groups (i.e., the assertive group may also have reported a passive response and the aggressive group may also have reported assertive and/or passive responses; Table 2). Overall, 75% of the aggressive group and 79% of the assertive group also reported using a passive response. Thus, students in all groups commonly reported passive actions. Just over three quarters (77%) of participants in the aggressive group reported using assertive strategies. Importantly, however, participants in the aggressive group reported fewer overall assertive actions than the assertive group ($\beta = 0.4$, $z = 4.26$, $p < .001$).

No significant differences were found on any outcome measure between the participants in the aggressive action group who only responded aggressively and those who used both aggressive and assertive strategies. This confirmed our categorization and analysis of students with an aggressive response as one group.

Action group differences

The random effects analyses tested the action group and school level variables while controlling for level of cyber-victimization experiences and gender (results in Table 3, with significant differences between action groups in Table 4). Student actions did not predict depression symptoms, SDQ

TABLE 3
Random effects models results for mental health and behavioural outcomes

	Level of exposure to cyber-victimization	School level (secondary)	Action group	R^2
DASS depression				
z/χ^2-value	5.2	−1.3	3.3	9.5%
Sig.	<.001**	.193	.189	
SDQ emotional symptoms				
z/χ^2-value	4.1	−2.3	1.0	5.4%
Sig.	<.001**	.020*	.593	
SDQ conduct problems				
z/χ^2-value	5.2	−0.20	17.6	16.1%
Sig.	<.001**	.838	<.001	
SDQ hyper-activity				
z/χ^2-value	1.1	1.2	27.2	9.1%
Sig.	.287	.249	<.001	
SDQ peer problems				
z/χ^2-value	7.7	−2.3	1.0	16.6%
Sig.	<.001**	.024*	.619	
SDQ prosocial behaviour				
z/χ^2-value	−2.8	−1.7	19.5	16.2%
Sig.	.005**	.091	<.001	
SDQ total difficulty				
z/χ^2-value	6.4	−1.4	12.6	15.0%
Sig.	<.001**	.170	.002	

Notes: Gender included as a factor in models to control for confounding—results not presented. Multi-category action group variable tested with likelihood ratio chi-square test, z-tests used for other factors and covariates.

TABLE 4
Raw mean scores[†] for mental health and emotional symptoms by "action taken"
groups

Action taken after cyber-victimization		DASS depression	SDQ emotional symptoms (5 items)	SDQ conduct problems (5 items)	SDQ hyperactivity (5 items)	SDQ peer problems (5 items)	SDQ prosocial behaviour (5 items)	SDQ total difficulty (20 items)
Passive	Mean	7.95	3.58	2.50	4.73[a]	2.10	6.97[a]	12.95
	N	60	62	62	62	62	62	62
	SD	10.46	2.55	2.02	2.16	1.77	2.13	5.44
Assertive	Mean	8.75	3.37	2.30[b]	4.19[a,b]	2.37	7.77[a,b]	12.21[b]
	N	231	243	243	243	243	243	243
	SD	9.56	2.51	1.72	2.14	1.88	1.94	5.54
Aggressive	Mean	11.41	3.71	3.37[b]	5.48[b]	2.45	6.72[b]	15.01[b]
	N	158	167	167	167	167	167	167
	SD	11.56	2.62	2.19	2.16	1.93	2.35	6.45

Notes: [a]Passive and assertive groups differ significantly. [b]Assertive and aggressive groups differ significantly. [†]DASS depression score range 0–42; SDQ scores range 0–10 for subscales, 0–40 for total difficulties.

emotional symptoms or peer problems. However, the type of action taken significantly predicted SDQ total difficulties. Participants in the aggressive action group reported higher levels of difficulties than those in the assertive action group ($\beta = 2.04$, $p < .001$). No significant differences were found for the other group comparisons—assertive versus passive ($p = .142$) and aggressive versus passive ($p = .317$).

In addition, the type of action taken was a significant predictor of conduct problems. Students who took aggressive action reported higher levels of conduct problems than those who took assertive action ($\beta = 0.82$, $p < .001$). The passive action group did not differ from the aggressive action group ($p = .104$) or the assertive action group ($p = .195$).

Type of action taken was found to be a significant predictor of hyperactivity symptoms. Students who took assertive action reported fewer symptoms of hyperactivity than those who took aggressive action ($\beta = -1.18$, $p < .001$) and those who responded only passively ($\beta = -0.63$, $p = .045$). No statistical differences were found between the aggressive and passive action groups ($p = .104$).

Finally, students who took aggressive action reported significantly fewer prosocial behaviours than students who took assertive actions ($\beta = -0.84$, $p < .001$). Students who reported assertive actions also reported engaging in more prosocial behaviours than those who responded passively ($\beta = 0.85$,

TABLE 5
Raw mean scores[†] for school level (primary vs. secondary) by mental health symptoms

School level		DASS depression	SDQ emotional symptoms (5 items)	SDQ conduct problems (5 items)	SDQ hyperactivity (5 items)	SDQ peer problems (5 items)	SDQ prosocial behaviour (5 items)	SDQ total difficulty (20 items)
Primary	Mean	9.77	3.80[a]	2.77	4.50	2.79[a]	7.51	13.87
	N	98	101	101	101	101	101	101
	SD	9.86	2.49	1.99	2.04	1.99	2.21	6.17
Secondary	Mean	9.53	3.44[a]	2.69	4.77	2.24[a]	7.23	13.15
	N	351	371	371	371	371	371	371
	SD	10.68	2.57	2.00	2.28	1.84	2.16	5.95

Notes: [a]Primary and secondary school students differ significantly. [†]DASS depression score range 0–42, SDQ scores range 0–10 for subscales, 0–40 for total difficulties.

$p = .004$). As with all the other outcomes tested, the passive and aggressive groups did not differ ($p = .987$).

Primary versus secondary differences

The impact of school level was included in the random effects analyses (results in Table 3, significant differences indicated in Table 5). No significant difference was found between primary and secondary students for depression, total difficulties, hyperactivity, conduct problems or prosocial skills. However, secondary students reported significantly fewer emotional symptoms ($\beta = -0.67$, $p = .020$) and fewer peer problems ($\beta = -0.46$, $p = .024$).

Finally, primary and secondary students' actions after being cyber-victimized differed significantly, $\chi^2(2) = 8.7$, $p = .013$, proportionally more primary students (64%) were categorized in the assertive group compared with secondary students (48%), while the secondary students were more likely to respond aggressively (38% vs. 25%, respectively). Similar percentages reported a passive response (11% vs. 14%, respectively).

Effect of level of cyber-victimization

As expected, the level of cyber-victimization was a significant predictor of each of the outcomes (Table 3) except for hyperactivity, with more experiences of cyber-victimization associated with higher levels of depression, total difficulties, emotional symptoms, conduct problems, peer problems and lower prosocial skills.

DISCUSSION

Appropriate coping and social problem solving (SPS) skills are necessary to effectively respond to bullying victimization, and impairments in these domains have been associated with mental-health problems in victimized students (Cassidy & Taylor, 2005; Warden & MacKinnon, 2003). This study examined the relationship between self-reported actions (aggressive, assertive, passive) after cyber-victimization and mental-health and behavioural problems.

While the type of action did not predict self-reported depression symptoms, cyber-victimized students who responded aggressively reported more overall difficulties, more conduct problems, more hyperactivity and fewer prosocial behaviours than students who responded assertively. Furthermore, students who responded assertively reported more prosocial behaviours and less hyperactivity than students who responded passively only. The lack of a relationship between reactions to cyber-victimization and mental health was interesting and unexpected. Perren and colleagues (Perren et al., 2010) reported that being cyber-victimized independently added to depression symptoms suggesting that cyber-victimization can be more challenging for young people. The results of this study suggest that student reactions to cyber-victimization were not associated with mental health symptoms indicating that the actions that young people engaged in after cyber-victimization did not improve or worsen symptoms of depression. Clearly, more research is needed to better understand this phenomenon.

Several other important results were reported illustrating the importance of post-victimization student actions and associated coping strategies and SPS skills. For example, no statistically significant differences were found between students who responded aggressively and those who responded passively, supporting the suggestion by Cassidy (2009) that passive strategies may be examples of negative coping. As the level of victimization was statistically controlled for in all analyses, this finding was not the result of passive responses being used in response to less severe instances of cyber-victimization.

Furthermore, cyber-victimized students who used aggression also used significantly fewer types of assertive actions than the students who did not, suggesting the former group used a smaller variety of assertive strategies. Although it is unclear if there were premorbid differences between these groups, the differences in relation to the variety of actions reported highlights the need to teach students a variety of ways to respond assertively and non-aggressively to cyber-victimization.

Developmental issues

Differences between primary and secondary students who were cyber-victimized were found for emotional symptoms and peer problems, with younger students reporting more problems in both domains. Furthermore, primary students were more likely to use assertive strategies and less likely to use aggressive strategies than secondary students. These results were contrary to our hypothesis and could relate to the duration of victimization; if secondary school students were bullied more chronically (i.e., for longer than six months) they may be more likely to respond aggressively.

Typically, social cognitive functions become more advanced over time enabling young people to develop more effective, and recognize less effective, strategies to deal with negative social experiences (Feldman & Dodge, 1987). Given the nature of the study design, it was not possible to determine the temporal sequence of victimization experiences and actions (i.e., did students engage in aggressive actions after first trying assertive ones). However, if children develop ineffective coping and SPS skills, making aggression more likely if victimized, these experiences may entrench maladaptive response mechanisms, further limiting prosocial behaviours and promoting aggressive and inappropriate reactions to victimization.

Thus, early learning of effective coping and SPS skills might reduce the likelihood of engaging later in negative reactions to victimization experiences. This highlights the need to give young people opportunities to practise a variety of socially credible assertive strategies in cyber (and non-cyber) contexts in order that responses can successfully be used in response to victimization. This social inoculation approach may be most relevant for students who are most at risk for victimization (either as a victim or both victim and perpetrator). Thus, efforts to promote appropriate and effective coping and SPS skills should begin early to ensure they are well established before students move to secondary school or victimization becomes more chronic.

Strengths and limitations

There are several strengths to this study. The results of this study provide some insight into the complex and negative relationship between reactions to victimization and mental health and behaviour. It is, to the best of our knowledge, the first study to examine this relationship in the context of cyber-victimization. Furthermore, the results have implications for the timing, nature and focus of prevention and intervention efforts to teach young people effective coping and SPS skills, characterized as assertive strategies, to reduce the negative impact associated with cyber-victimization.

Participants who reported engaging in an aggressive behaviour as a result of being cyber-victimized also reported significantly more concurrent mental-health and behaviour problems. Thus, responding aggressively to cyber-victimization may flag the need for mental-health support. A further strength of this study is the finding that participants in the aggressive group reported significantly fewer assertive responses than participants in the assertive group, suggesting that providing victimized students with a variety of assertive strategies may offset the potential to engage in aggressive behaviours. Importantly, having structured opportunities to practise assertive strategies will enable students to use these more readily if the need arises.

A limitation of this study relates to the design; the data analysed were cross-sectional making it impossible to understand the impact that the actions taken had on mental health and behaviour. Additionally, it is unclear if the students who reported aggressive actions were premorbidly different than other students. The parental consent rate of 85% may have excluded students at high risk of bullying victimization and poorer mental-health outcomes. The impact of this potential bias on the associations measured in this study is unclear.

While only one item was used to measure aggressive action, significant differences were still found between participants who reported responding aggressively compared with those who did not. Importantly, the reliance on only one aggression item means that victimized students may have been engaging in other aggressive behaviours not listed; and thus the differences in mental health and behavioural outcomes found between the action groups may have been underestimated. Given the item structure, we were unable to control for the duration of cyber-victimization to know the pattern of actions taken (i.e., began passive or assertive then became aggressive the longer the bullying lasted). However, the action item asked only about the actions that students had taken in response to cyber-victimization in the previous six months and the level of exposure to cyber-victimization was controlled statistically in all analyses.

A final limitation of this study was the use of self-report questionnaires. Although these are the norm in cyberbullying research, there is the potential for differences in response patterns (i.e., the difference between people experiencing bullying behaviours and defining themselves as being victimized). For example, a number of students ($n = 219$) who reported being cyber-victimized (on the victimization items) gave a different response on the action item (i.e., "I was not cyberbullied"). Thus, these students were excluded and we examined only those students who reported an affirmative response to the action item (which asked what students did after being cyber-victimized). Report by others is extremely difficult for cyber-victimization given its covert nature and this approach is likely to have several limitations.

Finally, because student self-report victimization-only data were used in these analyses it is not clear if these students also concurrently or previously engaged in cyber-perpetration and/or specifically cyberbullied their perpetrator in response to being cyber-victimized. The aggressive action group for example, possibly includes students who aggressively responded by traditionally or cyberbullying their perpetrator. The one-item measure of aggressive behaviour limits our understanding of cyberbully victim behaviour and other types of aggressive actions taken and may therefore underestimate the negative health effects on this vulnerable group (e.g., Haynie et al., 2001). Further research is needed to investigate the types of aggressive responses used by students who are cyber-victimized.

In conclusion, aggressive strategies (compared to assertive and/or passive only) in response to cyber-victimization were associated with mental-health and behavioural problems. Students who used aggressive strategies reported using significantly less of the listed assertive strategies than their peers who used assertive and not aggressive strategies, suggesting the need to develop and enhance students' non-aggressive social response repertoire to deal with victimization if it occurs. In addition, the difference between primary and secondary school students' actions in response to cyber-victimization highlights the need for early intervention strategies focused on the development of effective coping and SPS skills. The results of this study have important implications for prevention and intervention protocols and highlight the importance of early efforts to promote positive and prosocial ICT skills.

REFERENCES

Black, S., Weinles, D., & Washington, E. (2010). Victim strategies to stop bullying. *Youth Violence and Juvenile Justice, 8*(2), 138–147.

Camodeca, M., & Goossens, F. A. (2005). Children's opinions of effective strategies to cope with bullying: The importance of bullying role and perspective. *Educational Research, 47,* 93–105.

Cassidy, T. (2009). Bullying and victimization in school children: The role of social identity, problem-solving style, and family and school context. *Social Psychology of Education, 12,* 63–76.

Cassidy, T., & Taylor, L. (2005). Coping and psychological distress as a function of the bully victim dichotomy in older children. *Social Psychology of Education, 8,* 249–262.

Chang, E. C., D'Zurilla, T. J., & Sanna, L. J. (2009). Social problem solving as a mediator of the link between stress and psychological well-being in middle-adulthood. *Cognitive Therapy and Research, 33,* 33–49.

Child Health Promotion Research Centre. (2010). *Cyber-bullying: A definition.* (Available at: http://chpru.ecu.edu.au/)

Crick, N. R., & Dodge, K. (1999). "Superiority" is in the eye of the beholder: A comment on Sutton, Smith and Swettenham. *Social Development, 8,* 128–131.

Cross, D., Brown, D., Epstein, M., & Shaw, T. (2010). *Cyber Friendly Schools Project: Strengthening school and families' capacity to reduce the academic, social, and emotional harms secondary students' experience from cyber bullying (PEET).* Perth, Australia: Perth Child Health Promotion Research Centre, Edith Cowan University.

Cross, D., Shaw, T., Hearn, L., Epstein, M., Monks, H., Lester, L., et al. (2009). *Australian Covert Bullying Prevalence Study (ACBPS)*. Perth, Australia: Child Health Promotion Research Centre, Edith Cowan University, Perth.

Dooley, J. J., Gradinger, P., Cross, D., Strohmeier, D., & Spiel, C. (2010). Cyber-victimisation: The association between help seeking and mental health symptoms in adolescents from Australia and Austria. *Australian Journal of Guidance and Counselling, 20*(2), 194–210.

Dooley, J. J., Pyzalski, J., & Cross, D. (2009). Cyberbullying and face-to-face bullying: Similarities and differences. *Zeitschrift für Psychologie/Journal of Psychology, 217*(4), 182–188.

Feldman, E., & Dodge, K. A. (1987). Social information processing and sociometric status: Sex, age, and situational effects. *Journal of Abnormal Child Psychology, 15*, 211–227.

Goodman, R. (2001). Psychometric properties of the Strengths and Difficulties Questionnaire (SDQ). *Journal of the American Academy of Child and Adolescent Psychiatry, 40*, 1337–1345.

Gradinger, P., Strohmeier, D., & Spiel, C. (2009). Traditional bullying and cyberbullying: Identification of risk groups for adjustment problems. *Zeitschrift für Psychologie/Journal of Psychology, 217*(4), 205–213.

Haynie, D. L., Nansel, T., Eitel, P., Crump, A. D., Saylor K., Yu, K., et al. (2001). Bullies, victims and bully/victims: Distinct groups of at-risk youth. *Journal of Early Adolescence, 21*(1), 29–49.

Lively, W. J., & Bromley, D. B. (1973). *Person perception in childhood and adolescence*. Chichester, UK: Wiley.

Lovibond, S. H., & Lovibond, P. F. (1995). *Manual for the Depression Anxiety Stress Scales*. Sydney, Australia: Psychology Foundation.

Mayeux, L., & Cillessen, A. H. N. (2003). Development of social problem solving in early childhood: Stability, change, and associations with social competence. *The Journal of Genetic Psychology, 164*(2), 153–173.

Menesini, E., Modena, M., & Tani, F. (2009). Bullying and victimization in adolescence: Concurrent and stable roles and psychological health symptoms. *The Journal of Genetic Psychology, 170*, 115–133.

Perren, S., Dooley, J. J., Shaw, T., & Cross, D. (2010). Being victimized in school and cyberspace: Associations with depressive symptoms in Swiss and Australian adolescents. *Child and Adolescent Psychiatry and Mental Health, 4*, 1–10.

Rivers, I., & Noret, N. (2010). I h8 u: Findings from a five-year study of text and e-mail bullying. *British Educational Research Journal, 36*(4), 643–671.

Smith, P. K., Mahdavi, J., Carvalho, M., Fisher, S., Russell, S., & Tippett, N. (2008). Cyberbullying: Its nature and impact in secondary school pupils. *Journal of Child Psychology and Psychiatry, 49*(4), 376–385.

Sourander, A., Klomek, A. B., Ikonen, M., Lindroos, J., Luntamo, T., Koskelainen, M., et al. (2010). Psychosocial risk factors associated with cyberbullying among adolescents: A population-based study. *Archives of General Psychiatry, 67*(7), 720–728.

Takahashi, F., Koseki, S., & Shimada, H. (2009). Developmental trends in children's aggression and social problem-solving. *Journal of Applied Developmental Psychology, 30*(3), 265–272.

Wang, J., Nansel, T. R., & Iannotti, R. J. (2011). Cyber and traditional bullying: Differential association with depression. *Journal of Adolescent Health, 48*(4), 415–417.

Warden, D., & MacKinnon, S. (2003). Prosocial children, bullies and victims: An investigation of their sociometric status, empathy and social problem-solving strategies. *British Journal of Developmental Psychology, 21*, 367–385.

Yeates, K. O., & Selman, R. L. (1989). Social competence in the schools: Toward the integrative developmental model for intervention. *Developmental Review, 9*, 64–100.

Index

www.ingramcontent.com/pod-product-compliance
Ingram Content Group UK Ltd.
Pitfield, Milton Keynes, MK11 3LW, UK
UKHW020348010325
455677UK00021B/346

9 781138 844865